# PRAY ALWAYS

# PRAY ALWAYS

*What the New Testament Teaches about Prayer*

## ANTHONY LEE ASH

LEAFWOOD
PUBLISHERS

Abilene, Texas

# Pray Always

What the New Testament Teaches about Prayer

Copyright 2008 by Anthony Lee Ash

ISBN 978-0-89112-566-2

Printed in the United States of America

Scripture quotations, unless otherwise noted, are from The Holy Bible, New
International Version. Copyright 1984, International Bible Society. Used by permission
of Zondervan Publishers. Additional quotations from the Revised Standard Version of
the Bible, copyright 1946, 1952, 1971 by the Division of Christian Education of the
National Council of Churches of Christ in the U.S.A. Used by permission.

Interior text design by Sandy Armstrong

For information contact:
Leafwood Publishers, Abilene, Texas
1-877-816-4455 toll free
www.leafwoodpublishers.com

09 10 11 12 / 7 6 5 4 3 2

This book is dedicated to the hundreds
who have heard me speak of these things,
and to whose reactions I have listened.
Also to my wife, Barbara, whose tough questions
help me avoid sloppy thinking.

# CONTENTS

# INTRODUCTION

It has been my longtime goal to write this book. Over the years, I have preached many sermons about prayer, taught frequent seminars on the subject, and often counseled prayer for those struggling with problems. Some years ago, I wrote a small book on the subject, intended for adult Bible study classes, which covered prayer texts in the Gospels. I hoped then to follow with a book on prayer texts in the rest of the New Testament. Though that original title is now out of print, some people have been kind enough to tell me it benefitted them spiritually. It certainly had its shortcomings (as the present book, or any book on prayer must), but I felt it at least had some value in filling a tiny place in the void my fellowship was experiencing because of a lack of devotional literature on the subject.

Now I am daring to write the book about which I have thought for several decades. Or trying to write, for I find I am stuck at the beginning—stuck, even though the work is outlined in my mind and on paper. I do anything else instead of writing. I arise in the morning full of good intentions, and retire at night vaguely guilty because I made no progress on the project that day. When away from home, I am excited about the project, but when home, I avoid it in any way I can.

Prayer is certainly a prime factor in trying to surmount this barrier. I ask God to help me understand and trust he has given me some insight. I know a partial answer to my paralysis is an innate avoidance of whatever involves prolonged mental effort. Most of us understand that. But I also am embarrassed to offer instruction about prayer to people whose experience of prayer far transcends my own. I take comfort in feeling that I am not alone. Richard Foster confesses a like inadequacy in his book, *Prayer: Finding the Heart's True Home*. And in his *Letters to Malcolm*, C.

S. Lewis confesses to his imaginary correspondent the pitiful weakness of his own prayer life. As I recall it, Lewis suggests that his letters might cause people to think him a saint, when in reality his prayers were something crowded to the margins of his life. And yet, I cannot compare my prayer life to these two. At least, I don't think I can, though I sometimes wonder just what a prayer is. Is it possible a Christian prays more than just in formal times of prayer? Can a life, or parts of a life, be prayers? I still ponder over that, and will return to the thought later in this book.

There is something else. The more I reflect on the subject, the more complicated it becomes. I am often made aware of this when reading what others have written. Human thought is, at best, severely limited. We are acutely aware of this when we extend it to its highest consideration—contemplation of the Almighty. Rebounding from this, we also recognize that powerful praying is being done by saints who are not troubled by such speculations. Is it possible to over intellectualize the whole matter? Perhaps it is, for the tastes of some. Yet our minds are God's gifts, to be used to reflect on him; to abstain from this is a failure of stewardship. So one must plunge ahead into places where the water is too deep, hoping God's grace will empower the strokes, help one avoid the dangers, and show mercy to the swimmer, so that survival, not drowning, is the outcome. Because of the hope that God can use even a highly imperfect offering (as he uses highly imperfect humans), I will pursue the task of writing.

Now that I have written these things I can proceed. But here I find another barrier. Before settling into the part of the book's outline where I feel secure, I want to write about prayers in general terms, and about the assumptions prayer involves. But I also wish to address an issue that troubles many of us: Why, if we know prayer is such a wonderful gift of God, do we not do it? Why, if Jesus pleads with us to ask, seek, and knock, do we not ask, seek, and knock? Why, if our needs are so great, and God's response is so gracious, do we choose not to pray? My dilemma is how to relate the divine promise and human reluctance in a meaningful way. For some of us, the road to a rich prayer life is not easy.

For those who struggle with the smallness of their prayer lives, I confess I have no easy path to improvement. It still must often be "grit your teeth and do it," or "force the time out of your day," or "pray on the run."

Why can't our conversations with our Maker be easier, more intimate? I do not know. Some day, I trust, they will be our ultimate desire and glory. For now we are sputtering along. I hope he is pleased with that. I think he is! When we recognize the enormous power tapped through prayer, we must pray as best we can.

For those to whom this problem is foreign and who get along with great success in their prayers, perhaps they need to teach the rest of us. But please don't give us easy answers to difficult problems, and please appreciate our struggles. It isn't that we don't want to pray, or that we fail to recognize our responsibility to do so.

If what we find in this book stirs us to significant reflections on our prayer lives, I will have accomplished one of my goals. If it stirs us to more powerful prayer experiences, I will have accomplished another. We must never forget that in prayer we open ourselves to the working of God's power. No human scale is adequate to measure the infinite possibilities that power can effect. In prayer, we move into a realm whose mysteries inspire our profoundest awe. Whatever we say, in prayer we are touching the edge of something that must always stagger our imaginations. So we proceed boldly, for our Lord has so bidden us, but we also proceed with deepest humility, for he has bidden that as well.

*What to Expect in This Book*

Let me state a series of governing concerns in this book.

1–Prayer is one of God's greatest gifts to his children. We can never overemphasize its importance and power or the need for Christians to pray without ceasing. At the same time, God's gift should be instructed by God's word. Otherwise there is danger of going in wrong directions in our pilgrimage with the Lord. Though volumes have been written about prayer and the many perspectives from which to view it, in this book, I am concerned with demonstrating what the New Testament teaches.

2–For reasons that I explain at the end of chapter four, I draw material from the New Testament, and especially from the Lord's Prayer as set forth in Luke 11:2–4. The Old Testament does offer valuable instructions regarding certain aspects of prayer, but for the *content* of prayer, the New Testament is our guide.

3–As God worked through the (divine) man, Jesus, so since, God has worked through humans. He answers prayer through humans. They are his instruments. Therefore, in our prayers, we should implore the Father to work through us, or through others, in order to bring his answers to bear. To avoid this is to opt out of our responsibility as the people of God. It is almost to make ourselves spectators, standing back to see what God will do apart from any human agency. It has a very pious sound to speak of God's action apart from persons, but it can easily lead to lethargy and noninvolvement.

The opposite extreme holds that God does nothing in response to prayers, so we are left with no more than human efforts in addressing life's needs. However, this view overlooks clear biblical instruction concerning prayer and ignores the Christian conviction that God does work in the affairs of men.

4–My study of New Testament prayer has convinced me that most prayer ought to ask God to change people on the "inside" (with qualities like love, insight, and peace). Very few passages relate to prayers on the "outside" (weather, victory, a parking place). Thus prayer is addressed to transformation of the human heart.

5–I am convinced that free will is the proper Christian perspective. This conviction conditions the subjects and manner of prayer, as we shall have frequent occasion to recognize.

6–The goal of prayer is to accomplish God's purposes, not just to suit human whims or desires. We do not dictate to him! It is a great wonder that he even allows us to make the requests we do make.

*How to Use These Chapters*

My hope is that this book can be employed in Bible classes, but I have made a mistake. Most Bible classes run for four- to six- or thirteen-week periods, but this book has nineteen chapters (including this introduction and the book's appendix). I would be delighted if any class should decide to study through all of them. But if shorter sections are demanded by the class schedule, perhaps the following will be helpful:

Chapters two, five, six, and fourteen through nineteen can be considered individually, making single lessons or combinations of lessons. Some of these chapters could easily be divided into more than one lesson, depending on the discussion generated.

For a thirteen-week study, I would suggest chapters three and four, then chapters seven through thirteen, since they all have a common core. Then these nine lessons could be supplemented by any four from the list above. Consultation of the table of contents also can guide readers in deciding what to study.

## Thoughts to Ponder

1.  How would you proceed if you were to write a book on prayer?

2.  Garrison Keillor, in one of his Prairie Home Companion broadcasts, speaks of an uncle whose whole life was a prayer. Is it possible for a life to be a prayer?

3.  Why do you think we find it difficult to pray?

4.  Is it wrong to pray out of a sense of duty?

# CHAPTER ONE

# DEFINITIONS AND DIFFICULTIES

Prayer may be something we do, but we often have difficulty describing it in exact words. "I know what it is, but I just can't define it," we may say. Perhaps a simple definition would see prayer as consciously addressing ourselves to God. In such an address, we may praise, or thank, or confess to, or complain to, or argue with him. We may make requests of him. We may express concerns for others, or for ourselves. We may pray audibly or silently. Body postures may vary. We may be in solitude, or caught in the web of a day's business. Our moods may be devotional or frenzied. Our minds may focus or wander. Our lives may be tranquil, or we may be facing crushing crises. The time we spend praying may be hours or seconds. The prayers may flow easily or sputter from us by fits and starts. But in all these situations, we are deliberately communicating with the Lord.

## ASSUMPTIONS OF PRAYER

Lying beneath the apparently simple act of Christian prayer is a host of assumptions. It may assist our understanding to list some of them.

1—We assume there is a God and that he is one. This means, first, that whatever psychological good the prayer does us, we are not simply flinging our words into emptiness. There is a Listener!

2–We assume this God is the absolute Sovereign and Creator. He made everything that exists and all is under his power. He sustains all life. Whereas in some polytheistic systems, different aspects of reality are the responsibilities of the different deities, in Christianity nothing is outside the Lord's control.

3–We assume this God will hear us. Indeed, he urges his children to address him (Matt. 7:7–11; Luke 11:9–13). One might imagine a God who is unconcerned with human affairs or who is inaccessible to humans. We might even feel, as did certain psalmists, that he has hidden himself from our pleas (cf. Ps. 22:1). But prayer assumes he is there and that he hears. He hears, not just in the sense of being aware that we have prayed, but in the sense that he is interested and caring. This sense, to Christians, is deepened and enriched as we consider the compassionate and caring Christ. God cared so much that he became man, even to death on a cross. How could one conceive of such a God not being passionately concerned about his creatures? Thus, through Christ our understanding of prayer receives special dimensions.

4–We assume that God is not only interested but that he also desires to respond to prayer. Beyond desiring to respond, he has the power to do so. So both his power and his willingness, or desire, are involved as he attends to us. Power and willingness must always be considered together. The question is never just what God can do, but rather what he wills to do. It is easy for humans to bypass God's intents as indicated in Scripture and assume that he wills to do anything his power can achieve. We must avoid the temptation to assume that what we want God to do is what he desires or intends to do. He may have the power, but what we request may not be his will.

5–We assume that God has his reasons for offering humans the gift of prayer. Those who pray should do so with an understanding of what these reasons might be. This point is so important it deserves further discussion.

People, in all places and at all times, have prayed to the god or gods in which they believed. They often felt it was necessary to give gifts to the higher power to insure hearing and response. Often, also, they employed special acts of dedication or purification to ensure access to or response from the deity.

Through the ages, there have been numerous conceptions of this entity to which humans have offered their prayers: spirit, material, or something in-between; personal or impersonal. The rituals connected with these prayers have often reflected the conception of what people believed their deity could do. Frequently, the concept of a god was not based on any divine revelation, but was in fact a god designed as men wished or imagined him or her to be.

All cultures, as well, have testified to answered prayers. Whenever a request is fulfilled by subsequent events, the claim of answered prayer can be made, whether that is actually the case or not.

## HUMAN-CENTERED OR GOD-CENTERED?

In this broad reflection on the entire span of human prayer, we see a severe problem again and again. It is a concept of prayer that is man-centered rather than God-centered. Man-centered prayer can still use God's name and be festooned with religious trappings. But when this kind of prayer is examined, it turns out that man's will (needs, desires, fears) is more important than is any plan or intent of the deity in allowing and answering prayer. In truth, God is seen as a "cosmic bell-hop" (to use J. B. Phillips's phrase) who responds when humans call and is then dismissed.

Popular theologies of prayer often begin from a man-based perspective, rather than considering questions like, "why does God give the gift of prayer?"; "how does prayer fit God's overall plan?"; "what does God wish to give or to withhold?"; "is prayer just to make things easier for us?"; "for what should we ask in order to fit into God's purposes (rather than "what can God do to fit man's purposes and needs?)?"; or "how do we distinguish what we need (in God's eyes) from what we want?"

When we remember how self-centered humans are and that even believers are tempted to let their selfishness come before their allegiance to God, we can see how easily the gift of prayer can be skewed away from God's intent. We are tempted to act selfishly with all that we touch and thus must be eternally vigilant. It is probably impossible to completely avoid self-centered prayers. But since this book will deal largely with the subjects of prayer (and especially of requests), we must keep this caution constantly in mind. I certainly think God would desire us to ask about whatever is in our hearts—but he especially would wish our requests to reflect his agenda first, rather than our own.

When we pray, we expect things to happen that otherwise would not happen. Granted, even the experience of having our prayers received by God is a magnificent blessing. Just to talk to God is a wondrous privilege, but the picture we are given in Scripture is of divine response. Changes do occur.

Wherever the human encounters the divine there is the problem of finite minds attempting to grasp the Infinite. So in the life of prayer, we expect a large area of mystery. We know so little and do not understand so much that we think we know. We must be careful what we believe and say so that the truth can prevail.

## What We Do or Don't Do

As we continue our journey, we find two roads branching out before us. One is the "what we believe" road; the other is the "what we do, or rather, don't do" road.  Before we progress down the "what we believe" road, we must travel the other for a bit. To do so is painful for many of us because it involves encountering a failure that troubles our hearts. That failure is the inadequacy we feel in our prayer lives. Prayer is easy to avoid, sometimes irksome, and at other times forgotten or ignored. We intend a set regimen of prayer but never set it in motion. Or we may start a regular pattern of prayer, only to let it lapse. Perhaps we pray only as a duty, because it is "required" of good Christians, and then we wonder if we have really prayed as God intends. We may pray but perceive our prayers as shallow. All of this is enormously frustrating and guilt-inducing. We may be convinced that prayer is of surpassing importance, yet we do not bring that conviction into concrete activity.

Those who do not suffer this problem may omit reading the next few pages. The rest of us may be helped by exploring some of the reasons for our failure. I have arbitrarily divided these reasons into "intellectual" and "personal" categories. First, let us consider the "intellectual" difficulties.

The reason for setting these forth is because most of them disappear once we have a proper understanding of prayer.

*Difficulty #1–"God already knows my needs and has a plan for me, so why should I pray?"*

Though God knows our needs, his knowledge does not guarantee that he will respond to them. Scripture constantly stresses the need for faith. God acts for those who offer themselves to him for that action. To put it simply, he likes to be asked. We should not assume we will receive without asking what God may choose to give only when asked.

Regarding God's plan for a life, we must take full account of the freedom of choice that God has given us. In a profound sense God acts as he does because man acts as he does. To obey is to be blessed, and to disobey is not to be blessed. God's plan for life is found in Scripture, but each person must decide whether or not to adopt that lifestyle.

*Difficulty #2–"I don't know how God responds to prayer."*

Prayer is something we can add to the long list of things we do or use without understanding how they work. My list would include computers, automobile engines, televisions, the human brain, the growth of a seed, congress, or our dishwasher. Your list may not be the same as mine, but you surely have one. In a sense, God's call is "ask, seek, knock," not "understand" (though he also expects us to use our minds as fully as we can).

*Difficulty #3–"I don't understand how the supernatural (God's answer to prayer) works in today's world."*

This is particularly troublesome to those in a Christian tradition that believes miracles, as found in New Testament days, are no longer being done today. This may be another form of the previous problem, but many of us have been reared with a secular world view that assumes there is a natural explanation for everything. And then, God's supernatural responses to our prayers may well appear to us as natural phenomena; however, that does not deny that God has genuinely acted.

Deciding which things are and are not God's answers to prayer is a dicey business. Such a decision is liable to one of two outcomes: one is to deny that a certain event was an answer to prayer, and the other is to be sure that the event was an answered prayer. We want to praise God for what he has done, but at the same time we must have the humility to recognize our limitations and not to make claims when we lack sufficient insight. Fortunately, we are called to pray, not to pass judgment on how God answers prayers, or about what constitutes an answer. We simply pray with the faith that he does answer.

*Difficulty #4–"When God has not solved the world's big problems, why should I expect him to be concerned about my small ones?"*

There are still wars. Humans still exploit each other in terrible ways. Crass materialism still controls so much human activity. Human rights are still grossly violated. Natural disasters still run rampant. If God has not attended to these major issues, how can he be concerned with my minor ones?

We set against this the scriptural assurances that God is concerned about the fall of a bird, the hairs on one's head, and little children. These bring up the matter of determining what the "big" and "little" issues of the human scene really are. Perhaps there is really nothing bigger than the response of a single person to God.

*Difficulty #5–"I am puzzled about what to ask from God."*

This difficulty is often triggered as a result of hearing persons pray for things that we deem inappropriate. For example, how can one conscientiously pray for a safe trip and then drive recklessly? How does one pray for "national leaders" to rule a certain way when the values of those very leaders lead them in other directions? How does one pray for the sick without knowing whether or not God will heal in each case? The more one's prayers respect biblical concerns, the less these dilemmas will trouble.

We are still considering hindrances to our practice of prayer, and the second sort of barrier to prayer I have labeled "personal." Often these hindrances are emotional, and to deal with them involves trying to understand why we feel as we do. When we are beset by these emotional barriers, prayer may be extremely arduous.

*Difficulty #1–Prayer has such a low priority in our lives that we cannot marshal the discipline to do it.*

We may recognize that we "ought" to pray, we may even have a sense of guilt because we do not, but our guilt is not strong enough to move us to action. We must raise the priority level of prayer in our lives; however, this is not a simple procedure. It may be accomplished by an act of sheer will ("it is important, and I will do it!"), by deepened understanding, or by the urgency created by a crisis. Regardless of the impetus, the raw fact is that we do what is important to us, and we omit what is not. How much does talking to God matter? Some people find help here by keeping a prayer list that can be consulted regularly and by having a specified time set aside for prayer each day.

*Difficulty #2–Prayer is not enjoyable.*

This is often true. Many things we do are not enjoyable but for various reasons we still do them. Did Jesus enjoy his prayer of desolation ("My God, my God, why have you forsaken me?") from the cross? Yet, if we are made to serve God and enjoy him forever, we cherish the hope that eventually communication with him will be our supreme joy. Meanwhile, we are often plowing hard ground.

*Difficulty #3–We may feel prayer is unneeded.*

Life is going extremely well without it. Our own abilities and resources have been more than adequate. Frankly, we can do it ourselves. We have been given opportunities and abilities and have used them to our benefit. To pray may seem a denial of the life of self-discipline and effort.

The lives exhibiting this self-reliance are often admirable ones. Yet our needs, often hidden from conscious view, are always as real as those total needs we had as helpless infants. It is better for those who are abundantly blessed to be thankful to the Source from which the blessings have come. And what happens when life turns inside out and one is crushed by some tragedy?

*Difficulty #4–We avoid prayer because of deep feelings of unworthiness.*

Our sins and failures loom so large that we are ashamed to bring ourselves into the divine presence (as if we are ever away from that presence). "How dare a person like me go to him?" Perhaps a besetting sin makes us think our prayers hypocritical.

But who can God hear if not sinners and failures? His greatest saints are often most acutely aware of their sinfulness. Prayer is like the Lord's Supper. Our wrongs are not a reason for us to avoid the Supper because

we feel unworthy. To the contrary, they are the greatest reason to be reminded in this weekly observance of who and whose we are. Remember
that an important part of prayer is asking God to forgive our sins. We
should be delighted to approach him in the company of the prodigal son,
Saul of Tarsus, and the thief on the cross. If we ever think we must earn
the right to pray by our spiritual merit, we have missed the very heart of
the gospel of God's love.

*Difficulty #5–My prayers do not satisfy me emotionally.*

Because God sometimes gives us emotionally thrilling prayer sessions,
we are deceived into thinking only prayers of that sort are valid. We
are crushed when our prayers are dull and humdrum. It is urgent we
remember that God's desire for our prayers and his promise to answer
our prayers are never contingent on the emotions we feel as we pray. If
we could weigh the worth of various prayers, it might seem that those
forced from us by a sense of duty and unaccompanied by emotional
prompting would be the most valuable, because they demand the most
for us to pray them.

*Difficulty #6–We may be hindered in prayer for fear that God will answer.*

What if we allowed God truly to take control of our lives? Could we
stand such a radical surrender of self will? Most of us may want divine
help some of the time. But we have those pockets of life where we
cannot imagine changing. Every prayer of submission probably involves
a touch of hypocrisy. Most of the time, we may not even be aware of
our reservations. We say we want to be like Jesus. But if we truly understand him, our hearts may belie our words. Our self-centeredness
is too ingrained.

What are we to do? We must remember that God understands us
perfectly. We have said that our requests for submission are never completely honest. But neither are they completely dishonest. When we ask
to be more like our Savior, God's answer is to move us a bit closer to that
ideal. Then the next time we pray we can be moved even more closely to
God's intent. So throughout life, God changes us from ignominy to glory,
and then from glory to glory (cf. 2 Cor. 3:18). The alternative—not praying at all—can only lead us in the wrong direction.

*Difficulty #7–We simply forget to pray, even after we have experienced remarkable answers to prayer.*

Forgetfulness is at the root of much spiritual failure (see 2 Pet. 1:9). The Bible emphasizes the importance of remembering, as with the Lord's Supper ("do this in remembrance," and cf. Deut. 6:4–6).

*Difficulty #8–The last "personal" hindrance to prayer may be the most common. It comes because of the feeling that God has not answered our prayers.*

This may also be the hardest to deal with. We prayed in faith, and our prayers were fervent, repeated, and came from the deepest recesses of our being. Yet they were not answered. The dear mate, or parent, or child, or sister, too beloved, too needed, perhaps too young, to die, did indeed die after all medical arts and sincerest prayers failed. It didn't seem fair. Didn't God promise to answer the prayer of faith? Then why hadn't he?

Being angry with God is allowable. Plenty of the psalmists were. God can take it. But anger is one thing and refusing the help God would give is another. One does not desert one's mate, or child, because of some severe disappointment, or some promise broken. How much more ought not we desert God.

Should we keep praying if it just brings disappointment after disappointment? Yes. God still loves us, even when it seems he does not. If the Bible affirms anything, it affirms that. For God to have become man and to have died on a cross for us and then to refuse to love us when we are experiencing tragedy makes no sense.

Now that we have made a long journey down the "what we do, or don't do" road, we need to return to the "what we believe" road.

## WHAT WE BELIEVE ABOUT GOD

Prayer is almost universally practiced. Perhaps more prayers are uttered from non-Christian hearts than from Christian. Thus the understanding of any form of prayer involves understanding the belief context in which it is found, as well as understanding the nature of the one to whom the prayers are directed.

Since we are concerned with Christian prayer, it is important to consider what we believe about the One to whom we pray. As we survey various options, though we are concerned about sound Christian theology, we also are interested in encouraging the reader to a close and honest investigation of exactly what he or she believes. One can easily enough repeat orthodox formulations. But once past those, what personal statements would we make as we closely monitor our own hearts?

Our discussion has brought us to the edge of an intimate theological consideration. What does each of us, personally, believe about God? The honest personal answer to this question should be significant in explaining why we do or do not pray, and in explaining the nature of our prayers.

If you are asked what you believe about God, you may readily give "orthodox" answers. But is what you say what you really believe? Is it what you would stake your very existence upon? Many of us may not really know what is in our heart of hearts regarding this matter. We have never searched in that secret place. But our actions, or inactions, have betrayed those secrets.

So reach within and bring up the idea of God that governs your life. There are many views that humans entertain about God. The following are some that contrast with the biblical view:

- The atheist denies any deity exists. You may think you are far from holding such a position, but remember that the practical atheist may not make the philosophical denial, but lives as if no God exists (as in Ps. 14:1).

- Some consider God to be finite, limited in some way.

- Some hold a dualistic world view in which two divine powers struggle for ultimate mastery of all that exists.

- Some believe in an impersonal force or power that permeates all, but to which we cannot pray.

- Some consider God powerful, and even able to answer human requests. But he is unconcerned with human needs and affairs. He is unconcerned and unwilling to respond.

- Some see him as a God who answers every request of everyone. Or, to narrow it a bit, as a God who answers every request of any one of his covenant people.

Let us answer the summons to some serious thinking about God. Of course, our understanding will not change who God is. But it can change how we relate to him. We must remember that no man has seen, nor has any mind conceived of, God as he is. The human intellect is too limited an instrument. Though he has revealed as much of himself to us as is necessary for our salvation, even this revelation must be by comparisons or symbols, or in ways that transcend the categories with which we are familiar.

When we ask about origins (doesn't everything have to have a beginning?), we are told he has always been, that his origin is at no temporal point, and that our concept, which demands a starting point for all that is, has no relevance for him. When we inquire about size and location, we are informed that these categories are meaningless. Since size implies boundaries, it cannot be a term to describe him who is all in all. He may be in the tiniest bit of matter, but the cosmos is also within him. Regarding location, we know he is universal, or transuniversal. He is everywhere and beyond everywhere.

He is the environment in which we live. He needs nothing. He is the source of everything. He does not need food or home or air or earth or water or any "external" substance. We are never away from him. If he were to completely withdraw from us, we would cease to exist, since our second-to-second existence is only possible by his sustaining power.

He is also timeless. Since he is the creator of everything, he has created time. God is not in time, but time is in God. Should he choose to submit to time's boundaries to relate to us humans, it is only for the sake of that relation. This should not lead us to think he has past, present, and future, as we do. As C. S. Lewis observes, he is too completely real for that.

Scripture, unlike philosophy, does not probe all the deep issues involved in thinking and talking about God. But it does show God in relation to man, acting repeatedly on man's behalf. He is an able, concerned God, who hears *all* our prayers and grants some prayers. He always acts in accord with his greater purposes and does the most loving thing for his children. This is the reality that should be planted in our hearts and from which our prayer lives should spring.

With this picture of God, we come to the end of the first part of our study. Once, because I was overly optimistic and not a little naive, I thought that when a person's idea of God was correct, prayer would come easily. Perhaps for some who are far advanced in sainthood that is the case. It has not been so for me, nor, I suspect, for many of you. I would hope that as our knowledge of God is enriched, our prayers would be similarly enriched. But the road is still rough and there still must be duty. However, if we build on the right foundation—the right understanding—the road takes us ever nearer the goal. And perhaps it does get smoother as we travel, at least some of the time.

Reference to duty in the preceding paragraph brings me to another approach to the problem indicated by C. S. Lewis in his *Letters to Malcolm* where he discusses the "irksomeness of prayer." He suggests that our reluctance to pray may be the result of our human nature. By this he means our sin. But he goes beyond that. He argues that as post-fall creatures, we struggle to concentrate on things that are neither perceived by the senses (he suggests potatoes) nor abstract (such as numbers). God is concrete, utterly real, but not perceived by sense experience. The reality, Lewis says, goes so far beyond man's sensual or abstract experiences and perceptions that we are unable to capture a clear understanding of it. Since prayer brings us into this realm, prayer is difficult.

From this, and other, considerations, Lewis says we develop the concept of duty. We often cannot pray spontaneously, yet we dare not omit prayer. Thus prayer is sometimes, even often, an irksome duty. The glory days, when they burst upon us, will present a different reality!

### Thoughts to Ponder

1. How would you define prayer?

2. React to the idea that the main benefit of prayer is the psychological good it does to those who pray.

3. What is the difference between selfishness and self-interest, as they would be reflected in prayer?

4. Do you think of additional assumptions lying behind prayer?

5.  Do you find other difficulties besides those mentioned in your prayer life?

6.  Can you identify with any of the intellectual or personal hindrances to prayer? Which?

# CHAPTER TWO

# THE PRAYERS OF JESUS

The primary intent of this book is to encourage you, readers, in your lives of prayer. Essential to that is an understanding of prayer. Our basic source of information is the New Testament. But much of the contemporary understanding of prayer comes from Christian materials that have arisen after the completion of the New Testament. Some of this material is good, some not so good. Some of the ideas commonly accepted on this subject are difficult, if not impossible, to support using the New Testament itself. So the New Testament must be the pole star from which we need to orient our personal and corporate prayers and by which we evaluate the many circulating concepts about prayer.

But to what New Testament text or texts do we turn? Many passages are prayers or refer to prayers, but they do not offer a comprehensive discussion of the subject. What instructions do we find from Jesus? Here our quest is rewarded, for in Luke 11:1–13 we find the most complete New Testament text on the subject.

## BRIEF OUTLINE OF LUKE 11:1–13

Let us familiarize ourselves with Luke 11:1–13:

He was praying in a certain place, and when he ceased, one of his disciples said to him, "Lord, teach us to pray, as John taught his disciples." And he said to them, "When you pray, say:

"Father, hallowed be thy name. Thy kingdom come. Give us each day our daily bread; and forgive us our sins, for we ourselves forgive everyone who is indebted to us; and lead us not into temptation."

　　　And he said to them, "Which of you who has a friend will go
to him at midnight and say to him, 'Friend, lend me three loaves;
for a friend of mine has arrived on a journey, and I have nothing to set before him'; and he will answer from within, 'Do not
bother me; the door is now shut, and my children are with me in
bed; I cannot get up and give you anything'? I tell you, though he
will not get up and give him anything because he is his friend, yet
because of his importunity he will rise and give him whatever he
needs. And I tell you, Ask, and it will be given you; seek, and you
will find; knock, and it will be opened to you. For everyone who
asks receives, and he who seeks finds, and to him who knocks it
will be opened. What father among you, if his son asks for a fish,
will instead of a fish give him a serpent; or if he asks for an egg,
will give him a scorpion? If you then, who are evil, know how to
give good gifts to your children, how much more will the heavenly Father give the Holy Spirit to those who ask him!"

Two parts of this passage are also found in the Sermon on the Mount
(Matt. 6:9–13; 7:7–12). However, the story of the friend at midnight
(11:5–8) appears only in Luke. Because of the fullness of the passage, and
because Luke is preeminently the Gospel of prayer, Luke 11:1–13 will be
our beginning point, and we will work outward to the rest of the New
Testament. It is in Luke 11 that Jesus answered his disciples' request to
teach them to pray and thus teaches us as well.

### JESUS AT PRAYER OPENED A DOOR

　　　We will take the elements of this text and trace them through the
New Testament, including a consideration of the prayer life of Jesus,
which is pictured so prominently in Luke. We will also notice the prayers
of Jesus in the other Gospels. Then we will turn to the disciples' request
to be taught how to pray. Jesus answered their inquiry by giving them the
Lord's Prayer (or, as some prefer to call it, the model prayer). This was the
basic prayer given by Christ to his people, and therefore it deserves careful analysis. Just what are the implications of Jesus' instruction? We must
also consider the remarkable invitation to prayer given by Jesus with the
equally remarkable assurance that the God who desires us to ask, seek,

and knock is also the God who desires to answer. Finally, Jesus associated the Holy Spirit with prayer (v. 13), and this invites us to consider how the action of the Spirit relates to God's answers to prayer. We hope that when these investigations are complete, we will have a useful theology of prayer from the New Testament. We hope, further, that our prayers will become more significant as we relate to the Father.

Our first focus on Luke 11:1–13 tells us that Jesus was praying in a certain place before his disciples asked to be taught to pray. These words should not be dismissed as incidental. They send us into the rest of Luke's Gospel to see how we find Jesus at prayer on other occasions. The search repays us richly, for not only do we find numerous references, but we discover Luke was often concerned to tell us of Jesus' prayers when the other Gospels do not. Furthermore, Luke also gives us several of Jesus' instructions about prayer, and some of the best known of these are also only in Luke's Gospel. Obviously, prayer was a major concern as Luke was guided in his writing. It was important to him, and he considered it a thing his readers needed. Perhaps their prayers and faith in God's power were lagging and needed encouragement.

Let us look first at the instances where Jesus was praying. (I encourage all readers to read each of these passages before reading the discussion.)

### 1–Luke 2:41–52

When Jesus was twelve years old he was left behind in Jerusalem and became "lost" in the temple. This story gives us insight into his character when he was on the threshold of adulthood. Though prayer is not specifically mentioned, his presence in the temple and his reference to God as "my Father" imply a context and a spiritual intensity that would have involved prayer. When we ask, "what will this boy be?" we must surely assume that prayer was important to him as he increased in wisdom and in favor with God (v. 52). Thus this text hints at what was to come.

### 2–Luke 3:21

The baptism of Jesus is recorded in all four Gospels. It identified Jesus with John and his work and served as the inauguration to Jesus's ministry. After this event, he was a public, not a private, person. A voice from heaven, citing Old Testament texts, identified Jesus as the suffering servant most fully described in Isaiah 53 and as the king of Psalm 2:7. Luke alone tells us that Jesus was praying as heaven opened, the Holy Spirit descended, and the heavenly voice spoke, and Luke thereby presents the prayer life of Jesus as central to his identity and ministry. The servant king would be a man of prayer. (Incidentally, just as Jesus' work was inaugurated with prayer and the coming of the Spirit, so the church began with prayer and the coming of the Spirit—Acts 1:14, 24; 2:4.)

### 3–Luke 5:16

Jesus moved into his ministry, preaching, and showing God's power and authority through his exorcisms and healings. In this text we are told that Jesus, having healed a leper, "would withdraw to deserted places and pray" (NRSV). This event is also only recorded in Luke. It may be understood either as what Jesus did just after the healing, or as what was his customary practice (as NRSV has it). Why should Luke write this other than to emphasize again the importance to Jesus of these prayer "retreats"? Even when surrounded by great crowds he would find occasion to withdraw. Perhaps the account is telling us that only through prayer could Jesus find the resources to carry on his marvelous ministry.

### 4–Luke 6:12

Only Luke records this "through the night" prayer. This is the only account of such an extended period of prayer in Jesus' life. (Though one may extrapolate a similar event from Mark 6:46. After feeding the five thousand, Jesus went into the hills to pray; not until the fourth watch of the night did he walk to his disciples on the sea.) Even a quick glance at these verses impresses us with the importance of prayer to Jesus.

But there may be a further reason why we are given this information. This verse in Luke is at a transition point. Just a few verses earlier were several clashes between Jesus and the Pharisees (5:21, 30–33; 6:2, 7—over forgiving sin, meal fellowship, fasting, and the Sabbath) and just ahead was the choice of the twelve (6:13–16) and the first main unit of Jesus' teaching (6:20–49—the Sermon on the Plain). Luke may be telling us that times of prayer sustained Jesus through conflict and opposition, and that through prayer he chose the twelve from a larger group. The section from 6:12–9:6 has been called the training of the twelve, since the choice of the twelve begins the section, and sending them out to preach and heal concludes it. This interpretation gives even greater significance to Luke 6:12.

Of course, Jesus continued to train his disciples after the events in 9:1–6. We can imagine Jesus might have carried various names to God as he sought wisdom in choosing those who would enjoy special fellowship with him and to whom he would give special responsibility. One of those chosen was Judas, "who became a traitor" (6:16). It is possible that at this point he appeared to be a good choice, and Jesus may not have known what would come later (as he did not know the time of his second coming—Mark 13:32). Or if Jesus knew the tendencies of Judas, he may even have been put in place so God could use him (without excusing him) to accomplish divine purposes. Besides the choice of the twelve, Luke may also be saying that the great teaching of Jesus (6:20–49) emerged from deep communion with God. Thus we have significant choices and significant teaching, both empowered and guided by God, and coming in response to prayer.

### 5–Luke 9:16

When Jesus fed the five thousand he blessed and broke the loaves and fish. This is the first time Luke records a prayer of Jesus which is also found in the other three gospels. Perhaps these texts imply that through prayer God's power was brought to bear in great ways–here in the multiplication of food. This episode is one of several in Luke in which meals figure prominently—likely in preparation for the institution of the Lord's Supper. Jesus' prayer also stressed God's provision of food, which fits another emphasis in Luke (cf. "daily bread" in 11:3).

### 6–Luke 9:18

This text, containing the "great confession," describes a major turning point in Jesus' career. Here again, only Luke tells us that Jesus was praying. Luke is obviously concerned to show us Jesus at prayer at the major junctures of his life. This text may also imply, at least in part, that Jesus' messiahship was made evident because of his prayers.

### 7–Luke 9:28

At the transfiguration—a remarkable and mysterious event—Luke again, and Luke only, pictures Jesus at prayer. In fact this text indicates that the primary intent of Jesus was another "prayer retreat." The transfiguration, then, was an unexpected, but highly significant, divine interruption. Jesus was changed, as his supernal glory shone through the "cover" of his flesh. The great confession (9:18-20) and the baptismal words (Luke 3:21–22) were confirmed by the heavenly voice, but here God added the words "listen to him." The reference to prayer may be saying that prayer has transforming power. Through prayer Christians become more Christ-like. Also through his prayers Jesus' true nature was revealed. Prayer, rather than being a religious accouterment, was basic to Jesus' nature (and so should be the nature of his followers). Jesus was also confirmed as the authoritative teacher, even above Moses and Elijah (who had disappeared), and this confirmation came to a man of prayer.

### 8–Luke 10:21–22

This is the first time Luke gives the text of one of Jesus' prayers. Jesus recognized the mighty hand of God in the mission of the seventy, and was grateful for the defeat of Satan this had accomplished. He saw Satan "fall from heaven" in connection with their work. Notice here, also, the relation of prayer to the Holy Spirit—a point to be discussed later. Jesus here addressed God as "Father," which recalls Luke 2:49 and anticipates the prayer instructions of Luke 11:2. Verse 22 is an amazing self-description by Jesus, which some scholars have dubbed "a bolt from the Johannine blue" because it sounds so much like the statements about Jesus in John's Gospel.

### 9–Luke 11:1-13

This section of Luke, which is one of the basic prayer texts, has already been addressed above.

### 10–Luke 22:17, (19)

These prayers of thanks are also found in Matthew and Mark. They were a standard part of the Passover, but have achieved special significance for Christians because of the context in which they are set. It is on the basis of these prayers that the church routinely prays over the bread and cup at the Communion.

### 11–Luke 22:32

Jesus recognized the tremendous crisis his passion would pose for his disciples ("you" in verse 31 is plural) and so he knew they were in dire need of the sustaining power of his prayers. In particular he interceded for Simon ("you" in verse 32 is singular) whose leadership qualities are indicated here. The same qualities are powerfully demonstrated in Acts. This prayer-announcement to Simon is one of a number of places where we learn the intensity of Jesus' concern for the spiritual survival and growth of his disciples (cf. Luke 21:8, 14–15, 19, 28; 22:40, 46) This is the first instance Luke records of Jesus engaging in intercessory prayer.

### 12–Luke 22:42–45

This agonized prayer is recorded in all the synoptics (cf. Matt. 26:36-46; Mark 14:32-42). Jesus cast his fate into God's hands, rather than attempting flight or resistance. The intensity of the experience is underlined by verses 43 and 44 (unique to Luke) as they tell us of the angelic strengthening. (See also Heb. 5:7, which says, "Jesus offered up prayers and supplications, with loud cries and tears, to him who was able to save him from death, and he was heard for his godly fear.") Yet even with the angelic aid, Jesus' agony continued, as verse 44 witnesses by its reference to the "sweat. . . like. . . blood." These prayers may indicate that Jesus at least thought escape from death was a possibility. Or they may just underline the horror of what he was to endure.

Jesus' immediate request was for the removal of the cup (to be spared suffering?). But his deeper prayer was for God's will to be done, and for strength to fulfill his place in it. It is important to note this, since it is not uncommon for contemporary Christians to see "thy will be done" as an "escape clause" uttered in case they do not receive what they request ("My desire was not his desire. Oh well!"). But in Jesus' case, this was no rationalization to justify divine inaction, but a recognition that God's purposes are ultimate, and that man's ultimate obligation is to submit to these purposes. It might even be said that "thy will be done" should be the prayer beyond all prayers for every Christian. This is a clear case of the recognition that divine power must operate in concert with divine intent, and not just in response to human desire.

### 13–Luke 23:34

There are seven sayings of Jesus from the cross. One, "My God, my God, why hast thou forsaken me" is found only in Matthew and Mark (Matt. 27:46; Mark 15:34). Luke may omit it because he wishes to avoid even any hint that God abandoned Jesus. John has three sayings (19:26, 28, 30), none of which is a prayer (unless "It is finished" be so considered). But two of Luke's three sayings are prayers, and all three sayings are unique to Luke. Besides this verse and verse 46, see also verse 42.

The words in the text at hand sealed all that Jesus had said about forgiveness with his personal example (cf. 11:4; 17:4). In a way they express the very heart of the gospel. They also express God's mercy toward human ignorance, which Luke stresses elsewhere (Acts 17:30). Is it possible to imagine the divine magnanimity conveyed by this prayer?

### 14–Luke 23:46

These were Jesus' last words before his death. He was citing Psalm 31:5. It is worth noting how Jesus' first words in Luke 2:49 ("Didn't you know I had to be in my Father's house?") and his last, here, give the measure of his life. All that happened in-between these two prayers reveal this same God-centeredness. They are like parentheses, encompassing and defining his entire career. Jesus' climactic commitment to God, despite what God and man had done to him, offers humankind the most powerful incentive to trust even when in the valley of the shadow.

### 15–Luke 24:30

The last of Jesus' prayers in Luke reminds us of his other meal prayers, when he fed five thousand and when he instituted the Lord's Supper. It is interesting that the two travelers recognized Jesus neither by appearance, nor voice, nor message, while they traveled on the road. Yet prayer and a meal, typical activities, opened their eyes. Here is another way Luke shows prayer as intrinsic to Jesus' nature.

All of the preceding texts record prayers Jesus prayed. But they do not exhaust what Luke says on the subject. Among other things, he also tells us Jesus spoke of matters that could be the subjects of prayer. The Lord's Prayer is the prime example here and will be discussed in more detail later. Beyond this, in 6:28 (the Sermon on the Plain), Jesus told his followers to pray for their abusers (as he himself did in 23:34). In 10:2, as he sent forth the seventy, he urged them to pray that God would send laborers into the harvest since the opportunity was a great one. In 21:36, as he spoke of woes and temptations to come, he warned his followers of the need to pray for strength to escape faith-destroying troubles. Luke both began and ended the Gethsemane passage with Jesus' injunction to his disciples to pray that they "may not come into the time of trial." We see that Luke depicts the special shepherding concern of Jesus, because Luke is the only Gospel writer who brackets this text with these admonitions.

## Jesus' Teachings on Prayer in Luke

There are two other texts found only in Luke that give prayer instructions. Luke 18:1–8 tells of a widow whose persistence was repaid. A judge, bothered by her repeated entreaties, finally granted her request ("grant me justice. . ."). This parable is prefaced by its point. Jesus told his listeners "about their need to pray and not to lose heart."

The second text, in 18:9–14, contrasts the self-centered, boastful prayer of the Pharisee with the plea for mercy by the tax collector. Here Luke uses these prayers to condemn pride and to teach humility. Though these points need to be applied to all of life, they stand in boldest relief in one's direct prayer approach to God.

In this overview, we have noted how often Jesus prayed, and at what critical points in his life he prayed. We have listened to his words of prayer, for others and for self. We have seen how prayer was an intrinsic part of his nature. We have also heard him instruct his followers in prayer. A review of the subjects of prayer shows him teaching that a follower is to constantly place his or her life in God's hands.

Luke's emphasis on the importance of prayer meets the reader almost immediately in the Gospel. In 1:10, while those at the temple prayed, God broke in by sending the angel Gabriel to Zechariah, a godly priest. Zechariah, frightened, was told not to fear and that his prayer had been heard (v. 13). In answer, God would bless Zechariah and his wife, Elizabeth, with a son, who would be John the Baptist. Thus the great redemption story in the Gospels begins with prayer.

These prayers are interesting, but Luke did not write them simply to relate fascinating stories. They should instruct and spur us to action. For one thing, they show us the nature of Jesus in his prayers, which is what led the disciples to request prayer instruction. Jesus was the perfect man, an exemplar of what God created man to be. His prayers show that to be human is to recognize needs—needs only God can supply. As one views the life of Jesus, one hears the call to be like him. If you are what God means you to be, you will have fellowship with him in prayer, and you will bring him your needs, recognizing your dependent status.

Another way of seeing this material would be recognizing that Jesus was opening a new perspective on life to his disciples through his prayers. Surely they were deeply impressed by what he was, did, and said. He opened a door to live life a different way, to show possibilities they had not previously recognized. This new dimension was surrounded by and infused with prayer; hence their plea, "teach us to pray."

This upward pull emanating from Jesus' prayers can have a profound effect on those who would be disciples. But there is also an unhealthy way to consider his prayers. We might be tempted to think, "If Jesus, being who he was, felt such a need to pray, then *how much more* do we, being flawed as we are, need to pray." Of course this statement is true, but it motivates in the wrong way—by inducing guilt rather than creating desire. Most Christians already feel some sense of guilt because of the inadequacy of their prayers. Increasing this guilt only aggravates the problem rather than solving it. We need to remember that however we define the perfection of Jesus, he was human, with human needs. His perfection did not deliver him from this. Let us see the life of Jesus, then, as a powerful demonstration of what can be, rather than as a shame-inducing condemnation of us because of what we are not.

The prayers of Jesus underline and reaffirm the view of reality in which God is sovereign and all life is under his control. Man without God is man malfunctioning; man with God is man empowered. Man is not the center. God is. Man's freedom of choice is properly employed when he turns to God absolutely, not when he turns away.

## JESUS' PRAYERS IN THE OTHER GOSPELS

Let us now turn to prayers of Jesus found in the other three Gospels, which can strengthen the case we have been studying through this chapter.

None of the other Gospels stresses the prayers of Jesus as Luke does, but the prayer, "My God, my God, why hast thou forsaken me," is are unique to Matthew (27:46) and Mark (15:34). This prayer allows us to see the Lord crying out in the seeming desertion by the Father—much as many of the psalmists cried out (these words quote Ps. 22:1). Perhaps one lesson of this heavy text is that when we come to places in life from which God seems absent, we are not alone. We know that God, whatever the appearance, never forsakes his own.

When we turn to John's Gospel, we see a bit more of Jesus' prayer life, and the impressions we received from Luke are reinforced. Note the following:

*1–John 11:22*

Martha came to plead with Jesus for her deceased brother. She appears to believe Jesus' prayers could reverse death's verdict, for she said, "I know that whatever you ask from God, God will give you." Jesus spoke to her about true life. Later, at the tomb, Jesus thanked God for hearing him (11:41–42) and spoke the words that brought the brother, Lazarus, back to life. That restoration to life was a vibrant demonstration of God's promise to give greater life through Jesus.

*2–John 14:13, 15*

On the eve of his capture, Jesus promised his disciples that they would do even greater works than he had done, since he was going to the Father. He said, "Whatever you ask in my name, I will do it, that the Father may be glorified in the Son; if you ask anything in my name, I will do it." He went on to tell them that he would pray to the Father, and the Father would send them the Holy Spirit. It was through this power they would do the greater things.

*3–John 16:26*

The Lord spoke of a coming day when they would pray to the Father who would hear them because they loved Jesus.

*4–John 17:1–26*

This extended prayer, unique to John, has three parts. In the first (vv. 1–5), Jesus prayed for himself. He began by asking for strength to endure the coming ordeal so that God would be glorified by his resurrection, and then he requested to resume his heavenly glory. He offered the second part of his prayer (vv. 6–19) for the apostles, asking God to preserve them through coming trials. He also prayed for their unity, for their spiritual experience (especially joy) to be deepened, and for their sanctification. In the last section of his petition (vv. 20–26), Jesus prayed for all believers, for the unity that would be a sign to the world of God's work in them and for their glorification, which they would share with him in his glory.

## Thoughts to Ponder

1. What do you think is the point of Luke's emphasis on the prayers of Jesus?

2. If Jesus was God, how do we explain his prayers? Was God talking to himself? Or should we suppose Jesus was fully human in his prayers?

3. Why would Luke tell us Jesus prayed at the baptism, the great confession, and the transfiguration?

4. When Jesus prayed in the garden, did he actually think God would deliver him?

5. How could Jesus have needs that God could supply?

# CHAPTER THREE

# WHY BE TAUGHT TO PRAY?

We might try to imagine ourselves in the place of Jesus disciples and consider how our lives would be impacted by knowing and associating with someone like him. Wouldn't we be particularly impressed by his prayers? If we can imagine this, we can see how naturally they, and we, would ask, "Lord, teach us to pray."

## PRAYER, OLD AND NEW

Our first glance at this question could produce a misunderstanding. The request could be understood to indicate that the disciples had never heard of prayer, and thus had never prayed. If that were the case, they would want instruction in this strange new act. But a moment's reflection shows us this was not their meaning. They were Jews, with Scripture and synagogue in their background. The Old Testament is filled with prayers, and so was the synagogue service. They would understand prayer very well. For what, then, were they asking? I am convinced they wished to be taught the *content* of prayer. This point is so important it deserves elaboration.

First, every religion has its belief system and its view of deity. The prayers of that system reflect these concepts. Differences between Protestant groups regarding prayer may not seem significant, though even their "what to pray for" may differ from group to group. These differences depend on the varying views of the sovereignty of God, the nature of man, the way God's plans for human lives work, and how God answers prayers for the sick. In some cases, differences may simply reflect tradition. When we come to the differences between Protestants and Roman Catholics, attitudes toward Mary, Jesus' mother, would unquestionably influence prayer, and there are other differences when we consider how Orthodox Christians approach prayer. If we look at groups generally considered neither Protestant nor Roman Catholic nor Orthodox, we see prayers that reflect the beliefs of those groups, but which are outside what mainline Christianity would consider its basic beliefs. For example, the Shakers, of a past century, would make different requests of God because of a different theology. Today, Mormon prayer would differ from mainstream Christian prayer because of the unique view of God held by the Latter-day Saints. The same might be said of many other groups. And when we come to non-Christian prayers, the differences would be even more pronounced.

This is not to deny that prayers of many of these groups could have commonalities. But the similarities do not obscure the sometimes radical differences at the hearts of the belief systems. A devotee of any religion who is serious about prayer would ask, "Given what we believe about God, man, history, etc., how is it appropriate to ask God to act?"

So the disciples were asking Jesus how to pray in terms of his Messiahship (confessed in Luke 9:20), his teaching, his revelation of God as father (Luke 2:49; 10:21), his miracles—in short, in terms of all they were seeing and learning. They recognized that a teacher would give prayer instruction in view of his teaching for they knew that John the Baptist had taught his disciples a prayer (cf. Luke 5:33). The prayer teaching of a leader could simply be a matter of where he put emphasis, or it could open up some entirely new concept. We are not told, for example, what John taught his disciples to pray. But if we can make assumptions from his teachings, we might suppose those prayers would focus on repentance, or on a national return to God, or on the coming kingdom. Given this understanding, the disciples basically asked Jesus, "What about you and your teaching?"

A change from the old and known is implicit in the disciples' question. There were certainly points of contact in Jesus' teaching with prayer as they knew it. But they sensed the coming of a new thing, perhaps best shown by the new concept of Messiahship displayed in Jesus' person. For this reason, Jesus' prayer teaching is a thing different from the past, and therefore we will not turn to the Old Testament to find appropriate subjects of prayer. There are several other reasons why Christians should be cautious when they turn to the Old Testament (especially psalms) for prayer instruction.

1–In the Old Testament, God's people were both a spiritual and a political entity, that is, a theocracy. Prayers that assume this theocratic perspective are not appropriate for Christians, who are part of a spiritual kingdom.

2–The practice of Israelite religion presumed the existence of the temple. Further, it had a set calendar of holy days and specific corresponding customs and prayers. The New Testament established that Christians are not bound to these practices.

3–With the exception of less than a handful of late passages, the Old Testament does not recognize an afterlife, nor does it speak of a general resurrection of the dead. Blessings and curses were for this world. In Christianity, the concept of an afterlife offers a whole different dimension of prayer.

There certainly may be prayer instruction to be gained from the Old Testament, but such instruction should reflect Christian theology, not those characteristics of Israel's theology that are not required and possibly not appropriate for Christians.

None of this is meant to deny that the Old Testament can afford a rich resource for a prayer vocabulary (cf. Ps. 51). This is especially true where Israelite and Christian petitions deal with the same issue. Second Timothy 3:17 affirms the value of the Old Testament for Christians. What I am arguing is that we perceive the proper location of that value. Just as the heavenly voice said "listen to him" on the Transfiguration mountain, so we will listen to Jesus to understand the nature of kingdom prayer.

## WHY BE TAUGHT TO PRAY?

But why be taught to pray? Prayer is not a thing that flows from us in an unregulated way, but is to be contained within God-indicated channels. Of course, we all know that prayers of an unregulated sort sometimes come from those caught in life's difficult places. Sometimes they even come from unbelievers. On particularly critical occasions, it seems almost impossible not to pray. But these crisis prayers should not make us think prayer comes so naturally and automatically that we need no instruction. It is not uncommon for crisis prayers to cease when crises cease.

So why should disciples (past and present) be taught to pray? One reason is so we will pray for what matters in God's view of things. Who can deny that we often hear misguided or trivial prayers? But if prayer is God's gift, then to what end is the gift given? God, having made us, knows what we *really* need, and so he teaches us in the Lord's Prayer concerning these needs. There may be many things we want very much, or even think we need, but that God knows are not essential. He does not intend to answer prayers just to satisfy our whims or wants. God can do whatever he wants consistent with his being. The issue is not power, but will and intention. As an earthly parent will not give a child everything the child wants, so with the Heavenly Father. To build on Jesus' illustration, would you want God to give you a serpent if you asked for it? You might be bitten!

Part of the reason we are taught how to channel our prayers is that God, in his love, wishes to protect us from our own selfishness. All but the most saintly persons who pray fall into selfish praying. As hard as it is to say, some prayers for the sick are more for the one praying to escape pain than for the one for whom the prayer is made. Prayers that dictate to God may well be selfish. Into this category of selfishness fall prayers for victory (athletic, personal, or political), prayers for a romance to succeed, prayers for green lights and parking places, or, as in one extreme case, a prayer I once heard of for the molecular structure of an automobile engine to change (due to the owner's lack of repair money). But isn't God concerned about all our problems, even down to the pain of a stubbed toe? Of course. But is God to be glorified more fully by the cessation of pain, or through pain? Both possibilities can be documented from Scripture. On the one hand, we have the many healings recorded in the Gospels and Acts. On the other we have Paul's "thorn in the flesh," (2 Cor. 12:7–10), and the texts indicating suffering may well be part of the experience of Christians (cross-bearing, for example). Certainly we can carry all of our problems to God. But we must beware of a "big me, little God" philosophy of prayer. The glorification of God must be made paramount, not the glorification of man.

Another reason for instruction in prayer is so humans will avoid the tendency to bargain with God. During World War II, it was common to hear of promises made to God by combatants. "Get me out of this, and I'll serve you," or "Rescue me, and I'll do whatever you want." Out of combat has come the saying that there are no atheists in foxholes. The same sort of bargain has been made often through history. I can recall a number of old films where such a scenario was the climactic element of the story. But prayer is a gift of grace, as Jesus' teaching shows. Men never really bargain with God. They have nothing to offer him, save their decision based on their free will, and they only have free will because God bestowed it on them to begin with.

We need instruction in prayer so we will know God gives what he wishes to give, not what we have decided he wants to give. It isn't uncommon in popular books on prayer to read that we should visualize what we want until we are sure God wishes us to have it. Then we pray for our "vision" to be fulfilled. But this technique, besides being unbiblical, presumes upon God and can easily have us mentally putting him in the position of doing our will, rather than having us do his will (as modeled by Jesus in the Lord's Prayer).

Sometimes we interpret the invitation to ask freely in prayer (see, for example, Luke 11:9, 10) to mean that God will grant *any* request, as long as our faith in asking is of sufficient strength. We will speak about prayer and faith later, but I want to note here that every "whatever" passage appears in a context that defines the "whatever." In Luke 11, we find the context in verses 2–4, the petitions of the Lord's Prayer. And even if the specifics of God's answer are not set forth in the smaller context, they are specified in the larger context of the New Testament as a whole. That context, revealing God's plans and purposes, rules out views that teach that anything at all asked for in faith will be granted. God has checks on human folly and selfishness.

Is too much of a point being made here about harmless, but misinformed, requests? Perhaps, but it is a serious business to consider God as man's pawn, rather than considering man as a creature totally dependent on God and subservient to him. But there is another factor. If a person is convinced that God is present to do anything he or she asks, and that person prays upon that conviction, what happens if the prayer request is not granted? Rather than rescue, the outcome is failure of some kind. Though some people may handle these "refusals" with a certain resiliency, others are too brittle to do so. They become disillusioned, bitter, and cynical, and they may even abandon the Christian faith entirely. Short of such tragedy, they may never again have a full and satisfying prayer life. Because a faulty view of prayer had aroused faulty expectations, they had been set up for tremendous disappointment and spiritual tragedy. Better to be instructed about prayer and to ask for what God has promised to grant. We would do well to remember the aphorism that says "disillusionment is the child of illusion."

The fact is that everyone who prays has been taught how to do so, directly or indirectly, consciously or unconsciously. And I fear that many popular and well-meaning views of prayer do not conform to Jesus' teaching. A recent popular book on prayer, though offering many rich and inspiring insights, discusses prayer from the perspective of what people do and have done throughout history, rather than on the basis of sound biblical teaching. Thus much in the book is foreign to New Testament teaching, and some ideas flatly contradict Scripture. Some people get their concepts of prayer from the media, even from the Christian media. But shouldn't submission to Christ's Lordship and respect for the Bible dictate that we go to Scripture to learn about prayer? Shouldn't God's gift be defined by God himself, rather than being determined by human authority? Those who claim that the Bible is the only authority in Christianity should be eager to be taught by Jesus, rather than to be taught by other sources.

### Thoughts to Ponder

1. Have you observed differences in the content of prayers when comparing different religious groups?

2.  Can you give examples of prayers that tell God what we want instead of opening ourselves to his will?

3.  What kinds of prayers might be considered selfish prayers?

4.  React to the idea that we should visualize what we want until we are sure God wants us to have it and then pray for it.

5.  React to the comments in this chapter about the Old Testament and prayer. What about the use of psalms in prayer songs?

# CHAPTER FOUR

# THE PROPER ATTITUDES FOR PRAYER

L et us return to Luke 11:1–13, our basic text, and skip, this time, to verses 9–11:

> And I tell you, Ask, and it will be given you; seek, and you will
> find; knock, and it will be opened to you. For everyone who asks
> receives, and he who seeks finds, and to him who knocks it will
> be opened. What father among you, if his son asks for a fish, will
> instead of a fish give him a serpent; or if he asks for an egg, will
> give him a scorpion? If you then, who are evil, know how to give
> good gifts to your children, how much more will the heavenly
> Father give the Holy Spirit to those who ask him!

This divine invitation is only significant for those who exhibit certain attitudes. We now turn to these appropriate prayer attitudes.

Verses 9–13, in calling us to ask, seek, and knock, are calling us to faith. Why ask if we do not believe we are heard; why seek if nothing is to be found; and why knock on the door of an empty house? We must have faith in the validity of these activities, which means we must have faith in the one giving the invitation.

Faith is primarily the confidence that God will do what he says he will do, and that God can do what he wills to do. In the ministry of Jesus as recorded in the synoptics (Matthew, Mark, and Luke) faith is trust that

God can accomplish the miraculous. In the rest of the New Testament, the focus is on faith in Jesus and on the recognition that salvation comes through him alone. But the essential idea is the same. It is trusting that Jesus was who he said he was, and that he was and is truly Messiah, Lord, and Savior.

There is a further dimension of faith. Faith is the perseverance to continue and grow in such trust, when the assaults of life and the devil would destroy it. It is to be like the seed falling on good ground, growing and producing fruit many-fold. Further, why should we pray the Lord's Prayer unless we are willing to experience the personal change God's answer will bring about in our lives? If we have no desire for God's holiness to be manifest, why pray for it? If we have no sense of the offense to God constituted by our sins, why pray for forgiveness? If we will not forgive others, why ask to be forgiven? Prayer must come from a life of submission and obedience. Obedience to God, as we will see, has many facets, and often faith and obedience turn out to be almost the same thing.

## Faith

First, faith. The critical text is Mark 11:20–24 (parallel Matt. 21–22). In verses 11 and 12 Jesus had cursed a fig tree that was fruitless. This seems strange, since the text says it was not the season for fruit. Perhaps the tree, which looked good but bore nothing, was a symbol of Israel. That would fit the following passage: the cleansing of the temple. Some Jewish religious actions looked good on the surface but were corrupt beneath the surface. In connection with prayer, Jesus' condemnation came because the temple, intended for prayer, had become "a den of robbers" (v. 17). This can be contrasted with the statement about effective prayer in verse 24.

The next morning, the fig tree had withered, and the disciples' amazement drew forth these words from Jesus:

> Have faith in God. Truly I say to you, whoever says to this mountain, "Be taken up and cast into the sea," and does not doubt in his heart, but believes that what he says will come to pass, it will be done for him. Therefore I tell you, whatever you ask in prayer, believe that you receive it, and you will.

The power of God was underlined here, and that power could work through the lives of Jesus' followers. But they must believe in it. The text seems to be saying that the extent of divine action depends on the extent of human trust in that action. Yet it would be a complete denial of God's sovereignty and grace to say that faith *earns* God's action.

The affirmation regarding God's power and faith is so strong here that Greek uses the aorist tense (pointing to action in the past) to describe the receiving of what God gives. The idea seems to be that God's promise to faith is so sure that one can consider it already accomplished while one is praying for its accomplishment.

The relation of faith and God's power is found also in Luke 17:5–6, though this text makes no specific mention of prayer. The apostles requested of the Lord, "Increase our faith." He replied that the tiniest amount of faith (like a nearly invisible mustard seed) could cause a tree to be uprooted and planted in the sea. If minuscule faith could cause such a great unleashing of God's power, what might a larger faith do? Hence this call to faith hints at the great potential of prayers in faith.

To understand the instruction, "believe that you receive it," of Mark 11:24, let us examine some of Jesus' teaching about faith in Matthew, Mark, and Luke. Here are the texts, with an indication of what each says about faith.

*1–The paralytic (Mark 2:1–12; Matt. 9:1–8; Luke 5:17–26)*
The story of the paralytic lowered through the roof offers a surprise: Jesus' first response was to tell the afflicted man his sins were forgiven. All three accounts say that Jesus' words, and his subsequent cure of the man, came because he recognized the faith of the man and his friends.

*2–Two blind men (Matt. 9:27–31)*
The two men, crying for Jesus to have mercy were asked "Do you believe that I am able to do this?" When they answered, "yes, Lord," Jesus touched and healed them, "according to your faith."

*3–The sinful woman in Simon's house (Luke 7:36–50)*
Only Luke has this beautiful story of a woman, "who was a sinner," invading a Pharisee's mealtime and showing a remarkable love for the Jesus who could forgive her. After a devastating comparison

of the woman with the judgmental Pharisee, Jesus pronounced her sins forgiven. When others criticized him for this audacious statement, he told the woman, "your faith has saved you" (v. 50). She risked humiliation and rejection because of her conviction that Jesus could change her life.

*4–Stilling the storm (Mark 4:35–41; Matt. 8:23–27; Luke 8:22–25)* When Jesus' disciples were terrified by the violence of the wind-whipped Sea of Galilee, they cried to the Lord in panic. He awoke and chastened the sea as one might rebuke an unruly child. When nature obeyed his voice, Jesus (according to Mark and Luke) questioned the disciples about their faith. The story asks whether belief in God's power is such that it can accept his power operating even over the forces of dumb nature.

From each of these stories, and many others through the Gospels, we can learn something about praying in faith. Though faith acts, there is never a hint that faith "earns" a benefit. In each case, God's sheer grace was at work.

The call to faith in these stories seems, in every case, to be faith in the power of God. This power reigns over nature's forces. It invades the demonic realm and commands submissiveness. It intercedes in the God-man relation to forgive sin. It cures bodies cursed with epilepsy, leprosy, blindness, paralysis, and hemorrhaging. It reverses death's claim and restores life. The reality of these things seems hard to accept—until one recognizes the all-surpassing power of God wrought through Jesus.

We see even more potently the power of faith in these stories when we note the obstacles that believers overcame. They accepted as possible what their peers considered impossible. They persevered when discouraged or intimidated. They prevailed in the face of ridicule. The challenge in prayer is to cultivate powerful trust that God hears and answers prayer. These stories call the modern reader to go beyond the naturalistic limits our culture so often imposes and to then go boldly before the Father.

Let us now add an "exclamation mark" from James 1:5–8. James, more than any other part of the New Testament besides the Gospels, echoes the teachings of Jesus. In this passage, James trumpets the call to faith to readers troubled with stresses of various sorts. Their circumstances doubtless tempted them to question God and even to rely on themselves rather than on God for resolution. Such temptations have always troubled Christians when times are hard for them. In this context, we find these words:

> If any of you lacks wisdom, let him ask God, who gives to all men generously and without reproaching, and it will be given him. But let him ask in faith, with no doubting, for he who doubts is like a wave of the sea that is driven and tossed by the wind. For that person must not suppose that a double-minded man, unstable in all his ways, will receive anything from the Lord.

The call to faith was a call to trust God absolutely, to let his wisdom rule the day. God is reliable. Doubt makes us like sea waves buffeted by a stormy wind. Trust in God becomes a more difficult but also more powerful when born out of the actual pressures of life. We may not understand why life is as it is, but the call is not necessarily to comprehend, but to trust.

This call to faith cannot be issued too strongly. We should all cry, "Help our unbelief." It is in recognition of this that I offer two serious cautions to be recalled as we pray. The first has to do with the content of prayers that are offered in faith. In the texts with which we began this discussion (Mark 11:20–24; Luke 17:5–6), the point was the potential of faith. A misunderstanding of these texts, or of faith, would assume that *anything* requested in faith would be given by God. Not only does such an assumption go beyond the text, it simultaneously offers no check on human selfishness and raises the possibility of severe disappointment. Some would maintain that possession of faith opens the door in an absolutely unlimited way, but a bit of reflection will show that this view is mistaken.

All statements about faith and prayer must be set in the context of God's will and purpose. We can illustrate this from Luke 11:1–13. One might interpret the "ask, seek, and knock" in verses 9–11 as an unlimited promise, saying there is nothing God will not grant. But the context of prayer had already been specified by Jesus earlier in the Lord's Prayer (vv. 2–4). Thus the "ask, seek, knock" invitation applied to what Jesus had just said, and not to any whim or request that might enter the mind of the person praying. Any prayer asking God to help the petitioner hallow God's name would be granted, and we also can be confident in prayers for the coming of the kingdom, the dispensing of daily bread, the forgiveness of sin (as we forgive others), and the deliverance from temptations. To move beyond these loving boundaries may be asking God to act in ways that do not reflect his wisdom and love. We must remember that prayers center in God and his purposes, not in man and his wants.

Let us note in this connection three texts from John's Gospel that also sometimes are misused to justify the view that God will give humans anything they want. The texts are John 14:12–13; 15:7; and 16:23–24. John uses "belief" from a different perspective than does Luke. In John, belief is acceptance of Jesus' identity as he unfolded it to his followers. In these chapters, we have an extended farewell address, unique to John, in which Jesus promises the special gift of prayer. But we should note that in chapter 14, prayer was promised so Jesus' ministry could be continued through the apostles (v. 12), and it was to work to the glory of Father and Son (v. 14). In John 15:7, God's response would come to those abiding in Christ and in whom Christ's words were abiding. In John 16:23–24, prayer was to be in Jesus' name, which must certainly imply it must be within the parameters of Jesus' ministry and teaching.

We see loving boundaries in promises made in many areas of human experience. A Christian father may promise a child "anything he wants" as a birthday gift, but the child knows the promise must be within the context of the father's principles. He would not ask to be given a stash of illegal drugs, for example. Leaders in a church may assign tasks to the deacons, giving them free reign to do the job. But the deacons understand that whatever they do must be within certain biblical and ecclesiastical boundaries.

One more word regarding faith. We must be sure that our faith is in God. Though prayer is a mighty blessing, it is not faith in prayer that we seek but faith in the God who answers prayer.

A second caution has to do with emotions and prayer. A prayer of faith may or may not be a very intense emotional experience. Much depends on the circumstances, and perhaps even more on the emotional proclivities of the person praying. Some have intense moods, ranging far up and down an emotional scale, while others may operate on a more even keel. Our emotions are God's gift to us, and we are not all alike. Those of a more intense inclination may be tempted to equate faithful prayer with the production of a feeling believed to represent faith. But the value of prayer does not depend on our feelings as we pray. The danger is that we may strive more for emotional effect (the feeling we identify as faith) than for communication with God. Thus our focus would be upon our own internal psychological experiences rather than upon God. This, again, could easily make prayer self-centered rather than God-centered. There is another danger. Those of an intense emotional nature may be tempted to judge as invalid the prayers of those not experiencing the same emotions. Contrariwise, those less excitable emotionally may be tempted to judge highly emotional prayers as invalid.

C. S. Lewis speaks of "realizations" in prayer, by which he means this very thing. It is the striving to feel faithful, or courageous, or pious, with the presumption that the feeling is the same as the attribute, and that it thus validates the prayer. But Lewis cautions that the value of prayer does not depend on the emotions we can produce within ourselves as we pray. God is the one who decides how and why prayers are heard.

Please do not see this as a disparagement of emotional prayer. Our Lord wept and sweat a sweat like blood in the garden. But it was the circumstance that produced this awful anxiety. He was not trying to "get through" to the Father by manufacturing tortured feelings.

## OBEDIENCE

Let us look again at Luke 11:9–11 and consider the promise given there. We noted earlier that this promise is significant for those who exhibit certain attitudes. We have been talking about faith—the first of these attitudes. We now turn to a second. Prayers must come from an obedient heart. John 9:31 records the Pharisees citing a text from the Old Testament (Prov. 15:29; Ps. 66:18), and (mis)applying it to Jesus. "We know that God does not listen to sinners, but if anyone is a worshiper of God and does his will, God listens to him." Jesus was certainly not a sinner, contrary to the Pharisaic affirmation. Subsequent history of this verse has also been fraught with misunderstanding, as interpreters have defined "sinners" in ways to suit their own views. Yet the verse does express a truth. One living in sin, unaware of God, or not surrendered to him, may not even bother to pray.

We have already noted several texts in John (14:13; 15:7–8; 16:23–24) that depict the need for personal surrender. To these could be added

John 15:16, which speaks of bearing fruit in Jesus' name (cf. John 15:1–11). In 1 John 3:22, keeping God's commands and living as he pleases are essentials that create the context in which the Father responds to requests. 1 John 5:14 puts the promise God will hear in the setting of asking "according to his will." To these texts, we add 1 Peter. 3:12, which, quoting Psalm 34:15, affirms that the Lord's ears are open to the prayer of the righteous person.

Obedience can be seen from several perspectives, and the New Testament uses various approaches to this aspect of the proper prayer attitude. Prayer must be open to God and to his purposes, even if they run counter to human desires. Jesus, in Gethsemane, knew he could be delivered from the soldiers sent to capture him. God could rescue him by means of angelic legions. But Jesus knew this might not be the divine intent; he did not ask for such help if it conflicted with God's will (Matt. 26:53). I presume the preceding prayer of agony in the garden, asking God's will to be done, prepared Jesus for this sacrifice. The apostle Paul, tormented by a "thorn in the flesh, Satan's messenger," prayed three times for relief. Since he was submissive to God, he accepted God's refusal to remove the thorn and boasted in his weakness (2 Cor. 12:9). Better to be weak in God's care than "strong" outside it, for the former is the true strength.

We have already noted how humans are prone to act selfishly and how this corruption can sneak into the very center of our prayers. James recognized that fighting comes from coveting and lust and that such human passion operates at enmity with God (4:3). Prayer is to be couched in humility.

Who can forget Jesus' picture of the Pharisee and the tax collector praying in the temple (Luke 18:9–14)? "He also told this parable to some who trusted in themselves that they were righteous and despised others . . ." The Pharisee did not praise God, nor did he thank him. Neither, it is interesting to note, did he make a request of the Lord. Did he feel that God had nothing to give that he needed? Instead, he advertised himself before the Father, rattling off his own virtues. Even more reprehensible, he dared parade his own virtues by indicating the sinners from whom he differed. The crowning arrogance came when he disparaged a fellow petitioner by claiming he wasn't "even like this tax collector." Such a haughty spirit stands in stark relief to that of the tax collector. But it was not the sort of contrast the Pharisee imagined! The tax collector, who knew he was an undeserving bundle of needs, pled remorsefully for divine mercy. What a difference between pride and humility, focused at the point of prayer!

Just a step away from this scene, we find Jesus' words condemning showy hypocrisy in prayer. In Luke 20:45–47, Jesus warned about the scribes. He presented a powerful contrast between their pompous public display, calculated to elicit the admiration of those observing them, and their "hidden" behavior. This latter was of the most reprehensible sort, "devour[ing] widows' houses," taking callous advantage of some of the most pitiable and helpless members of their society. Then, to cover their wickedness, they "for a pretense make long prayers." How shameful to use an act indicating devotion and submission to God to conceal the service of Satan! What a classic case of profaning the holy. But Jesus saw through their blasphemous ruse, saying, "They will receive the greater condemnation." Prayer must issue sincerely from an earnest heart.

Before this condemnation in Luke 20, the Lord had issued other warnings against hypocritical prayer. In the Sermon on the Mount, he taught, "Beware of practicing your piety before men in order to be seen by them . . ." (Matt. 6:1); in Matthew 6:5–6, he spoke against public prayer done for display and insisted prayer be in secret. It would be foolish for one "in secret" with God to practice hypocrisy (hence the folly of the Pharisee in Luke 18:9–14). Though such private prayer would not impress the public, it would enjoy the divine reward. The key to prayer here was not the public display of the act, but the obvious quality of the life of sincere communion with the Father. Notice as well that it was not public prayer as such that Jesus condemned but public prayer abused to impress men.

In both Matthew's and Luke's accounts of the Lord's Prayer, an essential goal of the petitioner was to receive forgiveness (Matt. 6:12; Luke 11:4), and in these contexts, it is clear that a person unwilling to forgive others must not expect to be forgiven by God. The same call to forgive is issued in other contexts (Matt. 18:21–22; Luke 17:4), but none is stronger than the story of the two debtors in Matthew 18:23–35. There, a man who was forgiven an incalculable debt refused to forgive a much smaller debt owed him. The one who received mercy refused to show mercy, and against this sin, Jesus issued a scathing condemnation.

Volumes could be written on this subject of forgiveness, but we must content ourselves with a few observations:

1. The command to forgive is sometimes an exceedingly difficult command to obey. We are tempted to ignore it in extreme cases, and then to rationalize our avoidance of it. We might protest that the offense against us was too great to overlook. We might protest that no one could be able to forgive if he or she had been harmed as seriously as we were. We might note that popular opinion would certainly not think it appropriate to forgive such horrendous sin. But Jesus' word still stands. Thank God the Almighty, who does not seek excuses not to forgive as humans are wont to do.

2. Our responsibility to forgive has its significance in the very heart of the gospel. Whatever horrible things have been done to us, they will be far less than the horror we have visited upon God that he is willing to forgive.

3. Forgiving in difficult cases may be a slow process. We may begin with the knowledge that we ought to do it but only find ourselves able to utter feeble prayers for God's help. Our first efforts may be sheer will, contrary to our emotions (which would prefer to hate). But the efforts must be made. It is disaster to surrender the attempt and to capitulate to hatred, recrimination, and the desire for vengeance.

4. Unwillingness to even want to forgive is evidence that God's forgiving grace has not really been appropriated in our lives.

5. None of us can forgive as completely as God forgives, and as we find ourselves struggling to forgive, we may be tempted to despair. But we can *want* to forgive that completely, and we can let that goal draw us. We must recognize God's grace, blessing us and helping us grow to be more like the forgiving God himself.

6. Forgiveness of others is not complete until it is accepted. This acceptance involves sorrow and repentance on their part, and those we determine to forgive may not have these qualities. However, it is wrong to use their impenitent hearts as an excuse

to withdraw our willingness to forgive. The forgiving spirit must always characterize God's people, even if the forgiveness is not received, just as God is always willing to forgive, even if humans do not accept forgiveness.

7. Forgiveness is not an easy tolerance of wrong, as if offenses do not matter. As we said above, forgiveness is only complete when accepted by repentance.

8. We must remember that vengeance belongs to God. He is able to administer absolutely fair justice. We cannot.

9. We do not earn God's forgiveness by forgiving others. Both are matters of grace.

## MEANINGFULLY AND INTELLIGENTLY

I will discuss forgiveness further in a later chapter, but for now, let us return to one final quality of a prayerful attitude, which is indicated in Matthew 6:7–8:

> And in praying do not heap up empty phrases as the Gentiles do; for they think that they will be heard for their many words. Do not be like them, for your Father knows what you need before you ask him.

Prayer should be meaningful and intelligent. The Gentile prayers noted in these verses were probably repetitions of prayer syllables intended to "overwhelm" God by their frequency. One thinks of spinning a prayer wheel, or clicking some kind of counter. Those who have labored in prayer when burdened by heavy concerns know that in such cases the same prayers for help are made again and again. This cannot be avoided when one cares so much. Even if one knows, intellectually, that speaking to God once should be adequate, we still multiply our requests. But it is not against such prayers that Jesus spoke here. Rote formulae, repeated without a real sense of what the words mean, were his concern. He made it clear that man does not persuade God by inundating him with these "empty phrases."

We find another approach to this problem in 1 Corinthians 14:13–19. The issue there was the abuse of the gift of tongues in the assembly. Paul, who was himself a gifted tongue-speaker, argued that prayer should be offered with both the spirit and the mind. If it was unintelligible, it should not be practiced, since it would not edify the congregation.

Nor is the point of prayer to give God information (Matt. 6:8), as if somehow the Almighty had missed something. A prayer is neither a sermon nor an exhortation, though sometimes prayers are employed to these ends. Prayers do not need extensive commentary on a given petition "so God will understand." Nor is prayer a forum for advancing one's political or even religious views. God knows our needs, and we pray about them because we deal with them only through trust in him (cf. a more extensive discussion of this point in chapter 18).

What are we to say, then, about the use of prayer as advice, encouragement, comfort, or commentary? These activities miss the essence of what prayer should be. They tend to bend it away from its true purpose to our own interests. Perhaps this is not always harmful. The important thing to remember is that what we pray should be sensible and that it realize God knows all that we can ever say. In short, it should be truly prayer.

The previous paragraph may evoke a protest. There are times, perhaps in the hospital or at the sick bed, where a prayer not only addresses God but is also intended to speak a helpful word to those present. It is hard to criticize such a practice. Perhaps the reason Paul told his readers of the content of his prayers for them was to do this very thing—to encourage and comfort them by giving this information.

### Thoughts to Ponder

1. Discuss the danger of thinking that faith earns God's favor.

2. Why doesn't God just bless us, rather than "requiring" faith?

3. Some say that if we have a strong enough faith, God will give us anything we ask, and that unanswered prayer is due to lack of faith. Comment on this.

4. Contrast faith in prayer with faith in God.

5. What are the subheadings of obedient prayer?

6. Comment about the necessity of repentance on the part of the person being forgiven.

7. Where might one see the "heaping up" of empty phrases today?

# CHAPTER FIVE

# PRAYERS IN ACTS

Before looking at what the New Testament says outside of the Gospels and Acts concerning the subjects of our prayers, first let us observe how Jesus' example and teachings were carried out in the early church. Since we saw that Luke was the Gospel of prayer, we won't be surprised to find its sequel, Acts, continuing the same emphasis. Luke makes it clear that the early church struggled and grew by God's power because its members constantly depended on God. Certainly, Luke was saying to the church of his own day, and, by extension, to the church of all time, that it is by trust in God and by the outpouring of his power that his work expands and faces whatever circumstances it might encounter.

If we can forget for the moment that the text of Acts is so familiar and imagine it as a story we are hearing for the first time, perhaps we will see how exciting a narrative it provides. Within its pages, we find risk, danger, suspense, struggle, defeat, and victory, as well as a large helping of the remarkable. If we look only at the texts that mention prayer, we find the following: a group of people who seemed quite unpromising and who had been severely traumatized by the cruel death of their beloved leader. Then, beyond their despair came a rekindling of hope, accompanied by a strange promise of power. We find them waiting and wondering how this power would burst into their lives. We find them also faced with a staggering assignment of carrying the message about their leader and his teachings to the entire world. This was given to provincials who had probably never traveled more than a few score miles from their homes, who were not trained in theology or communication, and who faced a world in which communication over wide distances involved great expanses of time, accompanied by many dangers and uncertainties. These people, all Jewish but from diverse locales and with varied understandings of that ancient faith, were marked by an amazing unity, even to the extent of making extravagant sacrifices to supply one another's needs.

Soon after this new community—the followers of Jesus Messiah—was called into existence, they began to experience hostility from the Jewish religious leadership. They were unjustly imprisoned and forbidden to preach the message given them from God. Because they ignored this prohibition, hostility raged against them even more furiously, until the inevitable martyrdoms. They were forced to flee from their homes to safe havens, and even in some of those locales, persecution followed. In nearly every place the movement spread; it was welcomed by some but encountered virulent opposition from others.

Nor were the only difficulties from without. Serious problems threatened the internal affairs of the community. There were those who attempted to capture God's power for their own selfish designs. Then a great gulf was breached when the benefits offered through Jesus were made available to all men, not just to those within Judaism. This remarkable step, however, was not without friction. The early believers faced one of their greatest controversies over this matter, and the resulting tension persisted over a considerable time period.

It is an exciting story, and the episodes we have traced, as well as others, are punctuated, in Acts, by depictions of the church at prayer. As we have studied, Jesus had instructed his disciples in prayer, in response to their request (Luke 11:1–2). But nowhere in the Gospels do we find them actually praying. The nearest approach to it is Luke's statement in the last verse of the Gospel that they were continually in the temple praising God. But as Acts begins, we find them praying twice in the very first chapter, and frequently thereafter. After Jesus' ascension, the characteristic description of the apostles and other followers of Jesus was prayer. Thus, Luke was giving prayer as an identifying marker of Jesus' followers from the very beginning of the post-ascension period. Though the subject of these early prayers is not given, we might suppose it was for the promised coming of the Spirit (1:14, 24–25).

In one of these "prayer meetings," Peter presided over the group in order to select a successor for Judas. The man chosen, Matthias, is not mentioned again by name in the Bible. However, the early church deemed it important to have the full number of twelve in the apostolate, possibly to form a Christian correspondence to the twelve tribes of Israel. All the candidates, the church decided, should have been with Jesus throughout his ministry. When the eligible persons were determined, the matter was turned to the Lord in prayer. This is one of the few prayers in Acts where the words of the prayer are given (cf. 4:24–30; 7:59–60). Note their appropriateness. Those present addressed the Lord, as the heart-knower (a quality of Jesus often indicated in Luke), since they were asking for guidance in determining the internal qualities of the candidates. Thus the manner of addressing God was appropriate to the nature of the request, an example that can instruct us in making the way we address God more particular to our requests. Having turned the matter of selecting Judas's successor to the Lord in 1:24–25, the apostles determined his response by the casting of lots. We are apparently to understand that the result was not chance, but guidance. However, this is the last time indicated in Scripture where the followers of Jesus ascertained God's will through the lots, and we should be careful in treating this method as a relevant means of prayer today—after all, we are not given specific instruction on this practice, and it seems more likely that this was a cultural custom than an enduring spiritual discipline.

The end of Acts 2 presents an exciting picture of the church in its first days. Those who would emulate that community would do well to consider and replicate the qualities described in 2:42–47. In verse 42, one of four identifiers shown us by Luke as he opens the door of the church to let us peep in was prayer—in fact, devotion to prayer.

Soon troubles arose, and Peter and John were arrested. After an overnight imprisonment, they were hauled before the Sanhedrin. There Peter, filled with the Holy Spirit, countered his previous denial of Jesus (Luke 22:31–32, 54–62) with one of the boldest speeches found in Scripture (Acts 4:8–12), which he climaxed by "excommunicating" the entire Sanhedrin—unless they turned to Jesus. The enraged council, flabbergasted by this display of boldness, placed a ban against speaking or teaching in Jesus' name. After Peter and John's defiant answer, and further threats from the Sanhedrin, the two apostles were set free. They returned to a meeting of the believers, bearing the threatening mandate they had received. The response of the church was to commit the matter to God, the highest power, in prayer. In addressing him as "Sovereign Lord," they acknowledged his superiority over all earthly authority, including over the Sanhedrin. Then, invoking the second Psalm and interpreting it in terms of opposition to Jesus and to the church, they asked God to empower the church with boldness in speaking about Christ, as well as in the ministry of healing, signs, and wonders (cf. Acts 3:1–10). The place was shaken; God's answer was decisive; and the church continued its course, speaking with boldness about Christ. One might suppose that some of their number were frightened or intimidated by the forces arrayed against them. But God led them to rise above those fears. Acts offers encouragement to Christians in any age who may be stifled by fears and apprehensions.

Later the church was faced with its first internal dissension: a complaint by some Hellenists because their widows were neglected in the daily provision of food. Whether or not this matter had deeper causes, the problem could have seriously crippled both the inner life and the outreach of the church. The apostles, exhibiting great wisdom, delegated seven men of special qualifications to remedy the difficulty. The efforts of the seven, however, were buttressed by the prayers of the twelve (v. 4). When the seven were chosen, they were commissioned for their task by the laying on of hands and the prayers of the apostles (v. 6). Since verse 7 indicates further powerful evangelism in Jerusalem, implying the problem was solved, we conclude that the power of God was at work in the healing process. Here is another lesson for churches threatened with division: a call for more prayer and less acrimony in handling congregational problems.

Persecution became so intense in the case of Stephen that it led to martyrdom. Stephen, one of the seven "reconcilers" in the church, was also powerful as a preacher, and the force of his words enraged the Jewish leaders. The grim story in 7:54–60 tells of his death by stoning. But the grimness is alleviated by the victorious way in which he died. Like Jesus, who prayed for his executioners (Luke 23:34), Stephen prayed, "Lord, do not hold this sin against them" (7:60). As Jesus committed his spirit to God at death (Luke 23:46), so did Stephen ("Lord Jesus, receive my spirit"—v. 59). The reader is meant to see the parallel between Jesus and Stephen and to know how powerfully the claim of the Lord could work even on one in the throes of an agonizing death. One has no doubt that Stephen's prayer was answered.

Chapter 8 records a remarkable event. The Christian message left its exclusively Jewish context and moved into Samaria. There the gospel was received joyfully, as the conversion of the Samaritans moved a step closer to the offer of the gospel to all men. Would the Jewish churches, especially Jerusalem, accept this leap across the gulf between Jews and Samaritans? Peter and John went to Samaria and prayed for the Samaritan believers to receive the Holy Spirit. Incidentally, this event offers a remarkable contrast to Luke 9:51–56, where John had asked permission to bring fire down upon an inhospitable Samaritan village. Such was the power of the change wrought in John by God!

A notable Samaritan convert was Simon the sorcerer. He knew that his feats were nothing compared to the bestowal of the Holy Spirit by the laying on of the hands of Peter and John. Completely misunderstanding the situation, he attempted to purchase the power to bestow the Spirit on others. This impossibility was met by the sternest of rebukes from Peter, who made it clear that damnation awaited Simon unless he repented. "Repent" and "pray" were Peter's words. Simon, thunderstruck, pled with Peter to pray for him that he might be spared the threatened destruction (8:24). We have no doubt that Simon's initial conversion was genuine, but that his sin, prompted by greed, a lust for power, and ignorance, was terrible. The text clearly pictures both the gravity of the sin and the wonder of grace. The passage has appropriately been called the "plan of salvation for an erring Christian." Though the story of Simon is dropped after he asked Peter to pray for him, we believe Luke recorded this episode to give assurance that sinning Christians were not without hope.

We next encounter prayer in Acts at the house of Judas in Damascus. Saul of Tarsus, his life-direction shattered by a meeting with Jesus, is in agony and prayer (9:9, 11). Though we are given no specific indication, one imagines his prayers for God to grant him mercy and forgiveness, since of all the persecutors of the Christians, Saul was chief. It is common knowledge how powerfully God worked in this man's life. Like Simon, Saul was a sinner who knew the deep need for divine mercy.

Aside from the resurrection of Jesus, the most remarkable miracle in Acts may have been the raising of Dorcas from the dead (9:36–43). Peter was God's instrument. He was summoned to Joppa, where weeping widows offered touching evidence of the goodness of the departed Dorcas. Excusing all others from the room, Peter knelt by the corpse and prayed. As he did so, the mighty power of God brought the lady to life. Careful reading of the story notes the parallels to the raising of Jairus's daughter by Jesus (Matt. 9:18–26; Mark 5:21–43; Luke 9:40–56). Besides the significant connection of prayer and the unleashing of God's power, the text is showing how the ministry of Jesus continued through an apostle (cf. Acts 1:1, "began" in RSV).

Acts 10 records the great watershed event in the early church, as the gospel was offered to Gentiles without the necessity of their conversion to Judaism. The only condition to be met was faith in Jesus. The first Gentile convert, Cornelius, is depicted as a man of constant prayer (v. 2), and it may have been at such a time that the angel of God came to him instructing him to send men for Simon Peter. Likewise Peter, in verse 9, was also at prayer when God gave him a vision that ultimately led him to share the gospel with Cornelius and to his house (11:5).

A further crisis of persecution, this time from the Roman authority (Herod Agrippa II), is recorded in chapter 12. After the execution of the apostle James (12:1), Peter was imprisoned. As the story commences, we see Peter in prison on the eve of his trial or execution. The church turned to its greatest "weapon," earnest prayer (v. 5). When Peter was released supernaturally by an angel sent from God, he went to the house of Mary where the brethren were praying. The somewhat amusing sequence of events that follows, involving the maid Rhoda, indicates the reluctance of the Christians to believe their prayer had been answered. In recording this, Luke reminds the reader once again of the greatness of the working of God.

The second part of Acts, beginning in chapter 13, records the great missionary outreach involving Paul. The church in Antioch of Syria becomes central, since it was from there Paul was sent on his preaching travels. To that church, there came a divine word: "Set apart for me Barnabas and Saul for the work to which I have called them" (v. 2). The church obediently, with fasting and prayer, laid their hands on the pair and sent them forth (v. 3).

After a circuit of several cities in Asia Minor, and after numerous conversions as well as repeated danger and suffering, Paul and Barnabas returned to the cities where they had preached. They wished to discover the conditions of the churches they had founded and to encourage them in the faith. In fact, Paul's entire career was characterized by an intense and continuing concern for the churches where he had worked. So in Acts 14:23, we are told that besides the appointment of elders, "in every church, with prayer and fasting they committed them to the Lord." Whatever circumstances these churches might face, prayer gave them the ability to continue as God's faithful people.

These events took place on Paul's first tour. On his second, we see him crossing the Hellespont into Europe, specifically to Philippi. There, due to the jealousy of certain slave owners, Paul and Silas (now his companion in place of Barnabas) were thrown into a dismal maximum security prison cell. Unpleasant in the extreme, this circumstance must have been particularly wretched because they previously had received a brutal beating and now were forced into misery by being fastened in the stocks. One can hardly imagine the suffering of those hours. Thus it is remarkable that we hear them singing and praying from the depths of the jail (16:25). They subsequently were freed by God's intervention in the form of an earthquake, and though no explicit statement to that effect is made in the text, we might consider this a divine answer to their prayers.

As with the Gospel of Luke, there are fewer prayer references in the second half of Acts than in the first half. Beginning in Acts 20:1, Paul began his homeward trip at the conclusion of this third preaching tour, during which time he became aware that when he arrived in Jerusalem he would face "imprisonment and afflictions." Despite the entreaties of friends, he pressed on to the city, convinced that the Lord so willed. Indeed, his journey reminds one in some ways of Jesus' trip to Jerusalem in Luke 9:51–19:27. Given Paul's circumstances, his meetings with churches on his journey take on a certain poignancy of farewell. Acts 20:36 records his leave-taking of the Ephesian elders from Miletus, where they knelt in great sorrow and prayed together. Later, when Paul visited Tyre, a similar scene occurred as he departed, with Paul and his Christian friends kneeling on the beach in prayer as they bade each other farewell (Acts 21:3–5).

The next reference is retrospective. In chapter 22, Paul rehearsed his conversion before an angry crowd in Jerusalem. After his baptism and upon his return to Jerusalem, Paul had been praying in the temple and fell into a trance. Jesus spoke to him and warned him to flee from Jerusalem, telling him he would be sent "far away to the Gentiles."

It seems, as one reads Acts, that Paul would never achieve his goal of reaching Rome. One of the greatest hazards was the terrible storm at sea, which threatened to destroy Paul and all on board the ship with him. But it was God's will that Paul get to Rome, and so Paul announced that all on the ship would be saved for that reason (27:24). On the fourteenth day of the voyage, Paul urged those on the ship to eat. Then, as Jesus had done on previous occasions, Paul broke bread and gave thanks to God (27:35). This act could be called a sermon in prayer, since it called attention to the God whose power would save all their lives.

In one of the book's final scenes, survivors of the shipwreck landed in Malta, where Paul encountered the ill father of Publius, the chief man of the island. He laid his hands on him and prayed (28:8), and the man was healed.

If we draw all these references together, we can surmise what Luke is saying about the importance of prayer in the church. It is clear that this was an essential element from the frequency and variety of prayers noted in Acts. The first reference to the gathering of Jesus' followers after his ascension notes that they continued in prayer (1:14), and the first reference to their life together after Peter's Pentecost sermon specifies their continued prayers (2:42). The church was not simply a human enterprise: it was started and sustained by God, and in every aspect of its existence, the followers of Christ depended on God for the necessary resources to be the people he had called them to be. They knew that in his power, every eventuality could be met, and that he would see that his work continued.

As we can see from tracing prayer through the book of Acts, significant moments in the spread of the church came at times when prayer made openness to God's will most possible. If Luke's church read and understood, and if we read and understand, they and us are both taught to let life in God's community be constantly in "connection" with him. What an energizing picture Luke has given us in these texts!

## Thoughts to Ponder

1. Why do you suppose the Gospels never tell us about the disciples praying?

2. What do you think about addressing prayers to Jesus, in the view of the Father and Son relation?

3. How does the church today compare to the description in Acts 2:42–47?

4. Was Simon genuinely converted?

5. What is Acts saying to today's church about prayer? Do our prayers reflect the same kinds of needs and concerns as those in Acts?

# CHAPTER SIX

# HALLOWED BE THY NAME

Having seen the vibrant import of prayer in the early church, let us now return to the basic prayer text of Luke 11:1–13. Some years ago it occurred to me that the Lord's Prayer could be the basis for all the prayers in the New Testament. That is, everything we are told about praying for "something" matches one of the petitions in the Lord's Prayer. With this in mind, I read the entire New Testament to ferret out all the pertinent texts. Across the top of a page, I wrote the five petitions of the Lord's Prayer and then included each of the other New Testament texts where I felt it fit. I discovered that, exercising a little leeway, nearly all the New Testament prayers fit into this pattern. This made me think the early Christians may have begun with Jesus' instructions as they formulated their prayers. This led me to the conclusion that Christians in all times might do well to do the same, and that is the procedure we will follow here.

However, as I have reflected on the Lord's Prayer for many years, I have found that it has an amazing breadth of meaning. Thus I write with the recognition that what follows is only a little bit of what might be said. I hope this little bit is not skewed but is true to what God has given us.

Please remember what was said earlier. The petitions in the Lord's Prayer describe what we *really* need, and they caution us to avoid thinking we need what really is not essential. Plus, they warn us not to assume God will give us what he does not intend to give.

### FATHER

We begin with "Father"—the way Jesus told his disciples to address the almighty Creator. In the Old Testament, God is described in many ways, especially in Genesis (including El Shaddai, El Elyon, El Roi, and so on). In Deuteronomy 32:6, "Father" refers to God as the one who created and established Israel as a people and as the one who is the absolute Creator of all that is. Malachi 2:10 reflects the same perspective. The concept, then, is of power and authority. Other texts feature his tenderness and compassion (Isa. 63:15–16; 64:8; Hos. 11:3, 8). In some passages, "father" refers to the special blessings of the Davidic monarchy (2 Sam. 7:14). Still, using the term "father" for God is rare in the Old Testament.

What, then, did Jesus have in mind when he taught his disciples to say "Father"? Earlier, in Luke 2:49, he had spoken of the temple as "my Father's house" (contrast "your father" in 2:48). This usage from a boy of twelve may have been surprising. Then in Luke 10:21, Jesus addressed his prayer to God as "Father." This appellation, though known in Israel, was probably not customary, so that Jesus' usage is noteworthy. We might look at his granting this form of address to his followers as gift.

Of the various emphases that may be given the term, I prefer to understand "father" purely in the context of Luke 11:1–13. In verses 11–13, Jesus contrasts earthly fathers with the heavenly Father, who is a *giver*, and whose giving never will be mistaken or harmful. Matthew's text says he gives "good things" to those who ask (7:11). This view of God stresses his caring and kindness and conveys the idea of intimacy with him. If Jesus taught in Aramaic, as is likely, the original term for "Father" may have been "Abba," which was often a child's equivalent of "Daddy." Though this identification is not universally accepted, if it is valid, it conveys a marvelous picture of the loving care of the Almighty. Those who pray within the embrace of this intimacy can rejoice in the concept that he is the all-powerful Giver who will never betray or harm those approaching him in faith. Knowing God in this way is a powerful incentive to a life of prayer.

We will treat the succeeding parts of the Lord's Prayer as petitions. However, this leaves out the thanksgiving aspect of prayer, which is of great importance (cf. 1 Tim. 2:1). I would like to consider the address "Father" as implying thanksgiving, thus associating this aspect of prayer with the Lord's Prayer. A later chapter in this book will address prayers of thanks in more detail. God can only be a giver. We have nothing to give him. Even our decision to serve and obey him, which we tend to consider our own, is possible solely because he has made us able to make such a decision. So we are absolute receivers, and he is the absolute Giver. It is as Father that we see him most clearly in this role. Thus an implication of calling on him in this way is the clarion call to gratitude that it issues.

Though the concept of fatherly love and care was certainly a part of Israel's history, it received fuller explication by the way Jesus lived it out in his career and by its powerful manifestation through the significance of the cross and the resurrection. Christians, praying the Lord's Prayer after the resurrection, have powerful confirmation of God as an infinitely caring Parent.

## "HALLOWED BE THY NAME"

After instructing his followers regarding their special Father/child relation to God, Jesus told them to pray, "hallowed be thy name." In semitic thought, "the name" indicated the one named; so we might paraphrase, "hallowed be the God known as Father." "Hallowed" means to make or declare holy. Holiness, originally, referred to that which was set apart. God's holiness in this sense implies that he is unique, unlimited, Creator, Sustainer, Sovereign, incomparable. This prayer recognizes his very being, as much as it is possible for humans do so. In one sense, we can consider this phrase an ascription of praise to him. In thus recognizing his nature, it states the absolute reality on which all else rests.

Holiness later came to have a more specialized moral and ethical connotation. All human morality, from the Christian view, is a reflection of God's nature—his absolute purity and perfection.

To declare the holiness of God is to affirm the intended purpose of any act or thought. It is to affirm the purpose of a life, the purpose of history, indeed the purpose of the entire cosmos. All that is exists, ultimately, to affirm his holiness. Anything that is otherwise directed is a contradiction to the very nature of the Real.

So the first statement is a petition of praise. But as we think through the matter, we are led to ask how God, who is absolutely holy, can be made any more holy by our prayers. We know we cannot increase his perfection by our feeble expressions. What more, then, is implied by these words?

There is also involved here a petition—a request. As Christians pray, they are asking God to help them live his holiness through their lives. God is perfect; humans are not. But the more fully his people live his way, the more fully their lives practice and proclaim his holiness. This would involve words and deeds, but also the thoughts leading to them. The petitioner asks God, "Make me holy, so the holiness in my life will declare your holiness." Thus, when a holy life is lived on the human plane, and it is known to come from the individual's relation to God, those who see can affirm the holiness of the God who empowers human holiness. Thus, the prayer "hallowed be thy name" can be phrased differently as "help me to be holy, as you are holy." It is at the very least a prayer for divine aid in dedication and consecration to God.

We are asking God to help us understand him and his nature, since one's thoughts are parents to one's words and deeds. The more fully we understand, the more informed our prayers become, and thus the more complete the potential conformity to his being. But what audacity is involved in trying to understand the Almighty. Yet it is an audacity he bids us have and in which he aids us. Even such feeble progress as we make is wondrous beyond imagining.

In this process of prayer and divine answer, there is implied continual growth. Growth is sometimes painful. It is positively destructive to pride. It involves discoveries never dreamed of. It dictates change, sometimes even in the most protected areas of life. But with all its surprises and turnings, it is a great joy, as anything must finally be that leads us closer to our Maker.

Now let us search the rest of the New Testament for some other prayers that fall under the category of "hallowed." As we do this, it will be noted that many of these texts come from the prayer sections of the Pauline letters. Further, prayers of this sort make up a large portion of New Testament texts that indicate *the content* of prayer. This suggests to us that a major focus of prayer should be in the area of growth in Christ, a point worth noting when observing that many contemporary prayers seem to give this area of hallowing short shrift.

Many of these prayers are intercessions. We will discuss intercessory prayer later, but note for the present the conviction that the power in such prayer assumes a responsive attitude on the part of those for whom intercession is made. Otherwise such prayers would seem to be asking God to violate the free will of others, an unacceptable conclusion.

I have selected passages asking for spiritual and moral strengthening and deepening as exemplifying "hallowed be thy name." The interrelatedness of these prayers is obvious, though they are discussed here in no particular order. Further, if we were to develop these concepts beyond their inclusion as subjects for prayer, "the world itself could not contain the books."

## THE KNOWLEDGE OF GOD

In Ephesians 1:17, Paul prays for his readers that "the God of our Lord Jesus Christ, the Father of glory, may give you a spirit of wisdom and revelation in the knowledge of him. . . ." In subsequent verses this knowledge is focused on the Christian hope, the blessedness of being God's people, and the "immeasurable greatness of his power in us who believe." We will look at these topics more fully as we proceed.

In Colossians 1:9–10, Paul prays that his readers may be filled with the knowledge of God's will "in all spiritual wisdom and understanding," and that their lives may increase "in the knowledge of God." This increase is coupled with the godly quality of life that bears fruit in good works. A central theme of Colossians has to do with knowing Christ and what life in Christ means. Thus, we have a magnificent section showing the relation of Christ to the cosmos and to the church (1:15–20), as well as passages showing the hope that comes through Christ (1:27) and setting forth the fullness of life found in Christ (2:10, and see 2:2–4, 9–15).

The idea of "knowing" in the Bible implies much more than an intellectual, cognitive knowledge (though it does not exclude that). It involves the entire relation to Christ, its transformation of the inner person, new realities Christ makes possible in a life, and the quality of life flowing from the intimate relation with a God who is "Father."

Thus, in praying to know God, one is asking for a deepening and enriching of the entire Christian experience. Some fear that encouraging such prayer implies that there is revelatory knowledge of God to be gained outside Scripture. Yet there is room in every Christian life for a deepening of the personal experience of knowing and understanding what that relation to God means and how it is lived. Every Christian is aware that as the life in Christ progresses, one comes to further insights and understandings. The basic data of what God has done in Christ is complete and enshrined in Scripture, but the understanding and application of that message is a lifelong process.

Let us see the matter another way. None of us has completely mastered the biblical data. So we would have to admit we do not know all that has been revealed. But even if we had memorized the entire canon (even in the original languages), we still would not understand it all, and we certainly would not live it all. To grow, we pray so that God himself will bless and augment the process. Through what avenues does this happen? Through reading Scripture, obviously. Then meditation, memorization, association, conversation, Christian literature—all of them can be used by God. We remember that Jesus once used a child to teach a lesson. In the fuller awareness of the Father of our Lord, we are delivered from trivializing our faith and are called into the realm of ultimate and most earnest concern.

## APPROVE THE EXCELLENT

Paul prayed for the Philippians that their love would abound and that they would "approve what is excellent" (1:9). As one reads this letter and learns of the self-centered divisions in the church, one might be tempted to think some members had "approved" things inappropriate for themselves as followers of Christ.

As with the prayers for knowledge, here God was asked to act on the minds and hearts of Paul's readers. Their values needed to be centered in the right place. In Philippians 2, Paul places our focus on the mind of Christ (2:5–11; see also 1 Cor. 2:16). In the present context, approval of the excellent is a result of abounding in love, coupled with knowledge and discernment. The consequence of this approval results in pure, blameless, and fruitful lives, ready for the Lord's return.

The values people adopt lie hidden within their hearts. Though it may be possible to conceal their true nature from others, generally a person's behavior will reveal the person's values. Many things fill our minds—school, family, work, recreation, relationships, health, material concerns—and in themselves, these are not always bad. But the paramount value should be our relation to Christ, and all other concerns should be handled by that commitment. Often we are not even aware that other things may have displaced the Lord at the pinnacle of our hierarchy. So this prayer could involve asking God to assist us with self-knowledge. It also involves knowing the difference between the good and the best. As we know the excellent, we can make excellence our practice. This prayer shows again God's concern for the inner person. In that secret place, hidden from the eyes of others, the Christian life has its locus.

This emphasis in prayer can apply to any area of life. A good friend exemplified it when he prayed that God would give him a wife who loved God even more than she loved him. His prayer was answered in a wonderful way, by a godly wife who loves God supremely, and her husband in a splendid way as well. Perhaps both were praying to approve what is excellent.

### GROWTH AND IMPROVEMENT

All of the prayers in this chapter imply growth and improvement, but there are two texts particularly appropriate to discuss here. Paul concludes his letter to the Colossians with a series of personal references, one of which is to Epaphras, "who is one of yourselves, a servant of Christ Jesus." Paul reminds them that Epaphras was always in earnest prayer for the Colossians, "that you may stand mature and fully assured in all the will of God." Epaphras was likely the founder of the church in Colossae (1:7) and thus would have a special concern for these brethren. Though separated from them by many miles, his prayers bridged the distance with assurance that it was no barrier to the God who would help them cling more closely to Christ and deny the heresy threatening the church. Since the letter to the Colossians stressed the blessed wonder of life in Christ, I suppose Epaphras prayed that the truths Paul expressed in the epistle would seize and control their lives in a powerful way. Their own efforts to grow in Christ, then, were to be augmented by the power of God brought to bear through the prayers of their brother.

In 2 Corinthians 13, Paul concludes his correspondence by announcing that he was praying that they might do right (v. 7) even if his own efforts seemed to have failed, and he reaffirms his prayer concerns with the words, "what we pray for is your improvement" (v. 9). If we read 1 and 2 Corinthians and become aware of the many problems faced by that church, we more fully appreciate Paul's words. His letters, visits, and prayers show his passionate concern for these immature believers. If any group needed to experience the growth that God brings, that group did.

As we contemporize these prayers, it is with the recognition that even the best of us (and certainly the worst) needs to improve. The standard toward which we move is a perfect one, so that our quest and our prayers must never cease. It is arrogance for any Christian to think these prayers are no longer necessary. Growth is needed in concept, in word, in action. The possibilities are boundless. Remarkable discoveries of heart and life await the constant praying of this petition. Mature saints can certainly witness to the ways in which the experience of being in Christ becomes richer and richer as the years pass. Each time of life has its own problems and possibilities, and each needs to be surrendered to God so that it will bring the maximum blessedness and service for him.

## To Be Pure, Blameless, and Holy

The discussion of knowing God implies a quality of life. The Christian quality of life is what it is because of God's nature and his activity through Christ and the Holy Spirit for human salvation. We have already made reference to Philippians 1:9–11. Paul included in his prayer there the petition that his readers be "pure and blameless for the day of Christ."

A prayer in 1 Thessalonians 3:11–13 includes the request that God would establish their hearts "unblamable in holiness" toward him at the return of Jesus. Later in the book, 4:3–7 gives content to this petition with a discussion of sexual ethics (abstain from immorality; abstain from lust). And in 5:23, Paul prayed that the God of peace would wholly sanctify them.

Often Christians consider the development of Christian character, with its acquisition of virtue and avoidance of sin, solely a human effort. Christians try to be good enough to deserve God's blessings and then are in despair when they are caught in their inevitable failure. We need especially to avoid two errors: first, the belief that humans can achieve holiness on their own, and second, the assumption that if one prays, one need not make any personal effort to improve. Of course every Christian must try to be holy, but the point here is that what God asks from us, he also assists us in gaining. Moral virtue is a divine and human enterprise, and the role of prayer always should be recognized as of paramount importance.

## LOVE

Of all the qualities that characterize the Christian life, love is central. It most reflects the nature of God, who *is* love. Every virtue Christians are told to adopt and every sin they are to avoid is, when analyzed, part of the practice of love. The reader of Paul's great hymn to love in 1 Corinthians 13 learns that love is the ultimate quality, embracing all others.

Paul prayed that the Philippians' love would abound more and more (1:9). He prayed also for the Thessalonians, that they would abound in love "to one another and to all men, as we do to you." The practice of this love would create holy lives (1 Thess. 3:12–13). In this case we have confirmation of God's answer to the apostle's request. In 2 Thessalonians 1:3, written soon after the first letter, Paul thanked God that their love for one another was increasing—the very thing for which he had prayed.

But the pinnacle prayer to be loving is surely Ephesians 3:17–19, which says, "[A]nd that Christ may dwell in your hearts through faith; that you, being rooted and grounded in love, may have power to comprehend with all the saints what is the breadth and length and height and depth, and to know the love of Christ which surpasses knowledge, that you may be filled with all the fullness of God." Though there is disagreement about the exact meaning, it seems likely that the love in which they were "rooted and grounded" and which they were called to know further, was God's love for them. What a remarkable paradox is afforded by verse 19, with its call to "know" that which "surpasses knowledge." It is this knowledge that leads to being "filled with all the fullness of God"—a truly remarkable possibility. Whereas the Thessalonians references dealt with the love *practiced* by Christians, these in Ephesians deal with love *understood* by Christians. But the two are inseparable. The practice rests on the understanding, and the understanding surely must encourage the practice. To speak of either is to speak of both.

Love is the great motivating force in the Christian life. To attempt to live the life without knowing love can lead to legalism and superficiality. To know it produces not a complacent self-satisfaction but a sense of acceptance and security. A failure to know God's love can lead to unnecessary guilt feelings, destructive self-condemnation and misery. God knows what we are, how we struggle and fail, and he still loves us. Hence our prayers concerning love may well begin with a request that

God would help us understand its infinite and inexhaustible nature. The recognition of this grace produces gratitude and devotion.

Further, on a practical level there needs to be (1) prayer to help call love to mind as an operative entity in life's ebb and flow. Then, in perplexing circumstances, (2) there needs to be prayer to discern what is the most loving way to act in a given situation. These decisions are sometimes difficult and complex, calling for great wisdom. Then when the loving way becomes clear, (3) divine help is needed in finding the will and the strength to act appropriately.

In all this we recall, as we pray, that God loves all men, and so ought we. The New Testament speaks of loving God absolutely, of loving our neighbors, loving our brothers, loving the lost, and even loving our enemies. All of them are loved by God, even the vilest sinners and our most determined and wicked foes. This seems at times an almost impossible mandate, showing us again how much we need prayer to accomplish it.

## Hope

We already have had occasion to cite Paul's prayer in Ephesians 1. Recall that he prayed that God would grant his readers spiritual insight to know, among other things, "the hope to which he has called you." This hope, to be eternally blessed in the presence of God, is accomplished by the resurrection of Jesus from the dead and his session at the place of highest authority. It may seem at first glance that hope is so basic to the Christian experience that it is superfluous to pray for it. But anyone who has thought seriously about the matter recognizes the reality is so vast and unknown that prayer is appropriate to bring the truth more powerfully into one's life.

Life is so fraught with difficulties it is easy to allow them to dominate our lives. When we are thus dominated, we are led into despondency and despair. Hope lifts our vision beyond the unpleasant present and gives us a sustaining reality beyond the "valley of the shadow." Hope tells the Christian there can be no final defeat for one in Christ.

Enshrinement of this hope in the center of our lives (through prayer) imparts an optimistic quality to all of life. It abolishes the tyranny of the temporary by affirming the reality of the permanent. Since it is a transearthly thing, it also teaches us not to invest our ultimate confidence in anything on this earth, since such an investment is sure to bring disappointment.

Hope can be a powerful stabilizer and motivator. Christians who do not fully recognize it often stumble in their Christian walk. It may be argued that without hope, it is hard to see a reason to continue to live. But its presence colors all that we are, investing it with divine glory. This knowledge, further, is a thing that is so huge the human mind will never fully grasp it while in this life. Here is a country that will never be completely explored, though the forays we do make will reveal continued delights.

## ENDURANCE

In Colossians 1:11, we read, "May you be strengthened with all power, according to his glorious might, for all endurance and patience with joy . . . ." The Colossians were tempted by a "heresy" that included elements of Judaism, asceticism, and "worship of angels." Because our minds are not always focused on the ultimate, we too can be drawn aside to matters less important, or even palpably false. Thus the importance of endurance. Once we've made our commitment to Christ, staying with it for a lifetime can sometimes be difficult. Jesus, during his ministry, often showed concern for the endurance of his disciples (Luke 21:34–36; 22:31, 40, 46). Both in the New Testament and in modern life, we see instances of those who have not endured (cf. Demas, 2 Tim. 4:10).

Christians feel the force of the world, of heresy, of persecution, of fear, of lethargy, of rejection, and of many other threats to faith. Sometimes the alternatives seem more attractive than faith in Jesus. Many who read these words likely will have felt the tug of these or other forces. So, the prayers for endurance must themselves endure. They are prayed when we are so strong we think we can never fall, and they should also be prayed when we are on the edge and seem about to fall—when the prayers must be acts of sheer will, devoid of emotional support. And the God who does not change will answer and give sustaining aid, even when we may have convinced ourselves there was no hope.

## POWER

All prayer assumes a mighty answering power of God. It is imperative to recognize that Christianity is not a "bootstrap" enterprise, dependant solely on human will, energy, and effort. Unfortunately, there are

Christians who have this limited view. Because of it, they miss the full wonder of what Christianity is, and they are often dominated by a fear of God's wrath generated by knowledge of their own imperfections.

Among the letters of Paul, it is Ephesians that sets forth God's power most dynamically. We turn again to Paul's prayer in Ephesians 1:16–23, discussed in our above consideration of hope. The third thing the apostle asked God to give the readers was knowledge of "the immeasurable greatness of his power in us who believe" (v. 19). Paul shows glimpses of this power through reference to Christ's resurrection and his seat at God's right hand "in the heavenly places." There he is "far above all rule and authority and every name that is named" in this age and the one to come.

We stand in utter amazement before the wonders revealed in this text. As we pray for the operation of divine power in our lives, we are touching a force of incredible significance. Consider the following:

> 1–Paul goes beyond the limits of human language, and indeed of human understanding, with the expression "immeasurable greatness" of his power, a term that could refer to the mighty resurrection power that makes inclusion in the Christian body possible, or to the power available and operative in the life of the Christian to accomplish God's purposes there. Both are true, whatever Paul's intent in this text. Any sources of power, earthly or supernal, that the world has known or will know, if they are measurable, do not compare to the power made available in Christ, and through prayer.

> 2–Death, which seems so absolute, is itself a servant of God, for he forced it to his purposes when Jesus was raised. Man's greatest enemy becomes God's agent to his glory and man's salvation. This is how Paul demonstrates the power for which he prays (1:20–21).

> 3–This power is also manifest by Christ's role as head of his body, the church. The very existence of the church speaks volumes about God's love for humanity.

The act of a Christian in prayer, insignificant as it may appear, is a matter of considerable magnitude. In Ephesians 3:14–21, one of the most remarkable references to prayer in the Bible, we find important insight into the inner strengthening God can produce. This is the effect of the indwelling Christ.

In verses 20–21, Paul says, "Now to him who by the power at work within us is able to do far more abundantly than all that we ask or think, to him be glory in the church and in Christ Jesus to all generations, for ever and ever. Amen." The power working within Christians is beyond request or comprehension. Suppose a Christian begins praying a daily prayer for his life to be used by the power of God as fully as it is possible for it to be used. The person so empowered could reach levels of commitment to God undreamed of. Isn't this what we might expect from Paul's "far more abundantly than all that we ask or think"? What could Christians be as servants, teachers, evangelists, examples, in overcoming and enduring, as empowered by God, if they were willing to open themselves to the power? Unfortunately most hold back from such an amazing possibility. It may ask too much. But now and then we see someone who has accepted the challenge, and we are awed by what we see.

## WISDOM

James 1:5–8 offers assurance that God will give wisdom (generously) to those who ask. This request, however, is to be made from a life of constant trusting devotion to God. James describes wisdom further in 3:13–18, where he pictures it as a good life, opposed to "bitter jealousy and selfish ambition." Positively, it is a life that is "pure, peaceable, gentle, open to reason, fully of mercy and good fruits, without uncertainty or insincerity." The last qualities remind us of the warning against doubt and instability in James 1:6–8.

Wisdom requires reflection, observation, a weighing of data and options, and action based on an in-depth view of life's meaning under God. Wisdom is not polluted by impurities that confuse values. Wisdom strives for peace. It has an open mind to all factors and influences. It is compassionate, not insisting on harsh treatment before such treatment is warranted, and even then showing the mercy God would show. James concludes this text by a double reference to "peace" (3:18), which is a key component in the possession and implementation of wisdom.

If we extend the wisdom concept to the broader context of James, it would include, for example, appropriate use of the tongue, compassion for the needy, a faith shown in good works, humility, patience, etc. (cf. 3:1–12; 2:1–7; 2:14–26; 4:8; and 5:7–11). Wisdom is a quality that touches all of life. Parents, teachers, employees, employers, lawyers, police, coaches—everyone needs it. And all of us have a large enough fund of mistaken and ill-advised actions (even stupidities) that the need should be obvious. Is there any area of life where the prayer for wisdom is not imperative, and the promise of divine response a great blessing?

## Thoughts to Ponder

1. Comment on the idea that all Christian petitions in the New Testament spring from the Lord's Prayer.

2. How do you react to those who address God as "Daddy?" Why?

3. How do we make God holy (hallowed)?

4. Explain what "knowing" God and Christ means.

5. Can we have a knowledge of God that goes beyond Scripture?

6. Has your experience of being in Christ become richer through the years?

7. Would you agree that all the do's and don'ts in the New Testament are the practice of or failure to practice love?

8. Where in your life have you felt most keenly the need for wisdom? Where in your past have you failed in wisdom?

---

# CHAPTER SEVEN

# THY KINGDOM COME

After "hallowed be thy name," the next thing Jesus instructed his followers to pray was "thy kingdom come." Our first task in this study is to ascertain what these words meant in their original context; then we can proceed to contemporary applications.

## WHAT IS THE KINGDOM?

The Jews had not had a real king since Zedekiah, whose reign ended in 587 BC. Through the intervening centuries they had hoped God would send a Messiah and reestablish the Israeli kingdom. Then John the Baptist announced that the kingdom time was near (Matt. 3:2), and Jesus' central message was the advent of the imminent kingdom (Mark 1:15). The twelve and the seventy were sent out to announce the kingdom (Luke 9:2; 10:9), and the seventy were to announce it was near (Luke 10:9, 11). The populace expected a political kingdom, as in days of old, but the kingdom Jesus came to establish was spiritual. Consequently, those who came to accept him as king had to adopt a different interpretation of the kingdom.

There are two texts in Luke that appear to indicate the presence of the kingdom during Jesus' personal ministry. Luke 11:20 interprets Jesus' exorcisms as a sign that the kingdom was present. Luke 17:20, according to one interpretation, indicates the kingdom was present as Jesus was personally present. (See also Luke 16:16.) The rest of the texts in Luke speak of the kingdom in future terms. When seen in the light of Acts, this future may have been either near or remote. We might think of the threshold of the kingdom occurring in Jesus' ministry; the near future kingdom as fulfilled on Pentecost with the coming of the Spirit (Acts 2); and the remote future kingdom coming at the end time.

The nature of the kingdom can be surmised from the references to it in Luke. Jesus saw his death and resurrection as necessary for its full advent (22:16, 18). Thus, to pray for the kingdom to come was to pray for this startling fulfillment of Jesus' mission. In view of this, he called for the greatest devotion from those who would follow him, since he would be a suffering Messiah (9:60, 62; 14:15–24; 18:24, 25, 29). Those who accepted the challenge would be blessed in so doing (among other references, see 6:20; 19:17; and 23:42–43).

Jesus indicated the ethics of the kingdom in his Sermon on the Plain (Luke 6:20–49), with his central focus being love. There are also many ethical teachings in the "journey to Jerusalem" section in Luke 9:51–19:27. Together, these passages include calls to trust God absolutely, warnings about the potential corrupting power of wealth, and calls to humility.

Thus, to pray "thy kingdom come" involved a number of issues. There was a new understanding of the Kingdom of God, a recognition of the place of Jesus' passion in its arrival, a sense of what was demanded of those who would enter, and an awareness of the blessedness of that "citizenship." Followers of Jesus were to pray for God's rule to invade human affairs, with all that involved. In fact, the kingdom might best be defined as the rule or reign of God.

In Matthew's account, we find the additional clause, "thy will be done, on earth as it is in heaven." This may be a case of parallelism, in which the additional words restate in different terms the idea of the first words, which would give us the clearer understanding that God's rule is what takes place when God's will is accomplished among men.

Now let us consider the issue of human free will. In Jesus' day, and in all time to the present day, the rule of God can be fully effective on earth only where humans will allow it to be. People must be willing to open their lives to full trust in God. They must be willing to accept what Jesus has done and make a complete commitment to it. They must be willing to live the life required of those in the kingdom. In short, they must be "born again," that is, become Christians in the fullest sense. Whatever will be the nature of the final act of history, in this life God "honors" the right he has given his creatures to say "yes" or to say "no" to him.

When, then, does the rule of God come in human affairs? It comes when our "yes" allows it to come. To put it another way, whenever and wherever God's name is hallowed, there the kingdom has come. Thus, our primary contemporary focus on "thy kingdom come" will center on prayers that God's rule will come to lives where it has not previously existed—that is, we will focus on evangelism. Within this category, we will be chiefly concerned with God's action on the evangelist as he or she calls others to submit to God's rule.

## PRAYERS FOR EVANGELISM

The very word "evangelism" evokes different emotions in different people. On the one hand, there is the "high pressure" evangelist who never misses an opportunity to speak for Jesus and who uses various means to compel decisions. These people win some and alienate others. On the other extreme are those for whom evangelism forms no part of their Christian life. This may be accompanied with complete indifference, or, in some cases, with intense feelings of guilt because of a conviction that God's wrath will meet those who have done no soul-winning.

Here are some assumptions we make as we discuss this topic:

1. God wants people to be drawn into the kingdom, to acknowledge his rule. This is really the story of the entire Bible: God reaching out to his creatures.

2. God uses Christians to draw the world into the kingdom.

3. God will bless this process. The process and the blessing may take many forms.

4. Unfortunately, much of the emphasis placed on evangelism today works by guilt motivation.

5. Rather than seeing evangelism as a human work, we must see it as a divine work using human instruments. In other words, the place to begin the evangelistic process is on our knees, asking God to use us.

6. When God's rule comes in a human life, he will bring happiness, peace of mind, meaning, love, hope, inner strength, and purpose—all the things humans really need.

Let us begin with a personal inventory. This must be done as honestly as possible. How are you as an evangelist? Have you led anyone to Jesus? Have you even tried? When you scrutinize yourself in this regard, where do you see areas of need? Do you feel that your understanding of the Christian faith is so lacking that you would not consider trying to communicate it to others? Are you afraid that the quality of your commitment to Jesus is too weak for you to even begin trying to encourage others to have faith? Have you tried and failed to win others, with the sense that you had made matters worse than if you had said nothing? Do you lack the wisdom and insight to know-how to proceed in introducing others to the Lord?

Perhaps you are plagued by the shortcoming that has been my greatest hindrance. I want so much to be liked, and am so afraid of rejection and ridicule, that the prospect of speaking to someone else about Christ creates an enormous shyness. I am afraid that I might experience rejection, or be considered a fanatic, or become the butt of ridicule.

Are you interested in being evangelistic, but feel the proper times and circumstances never come to enable evangelism to take place? Or, when you have made the effort, have the person or persons whom you approached been obviously uninterested, or even resentful?

From my own observation, it seems that Christians have been urged to "win souls" without due regard to the hazards that keep this from happening. Such appeals do not result in conversions, but only in producing miserable, guilt-ridden Christians. It was against the background of my own great anguish over this dilemma that two insights proved enormously liberating. The first was the recognition that God never asks us to do anything he will not empower us to do. This opened the door to prayer. If I would pray, God would bless and use me in ways he saw fit. Evangelism was his work, and I was to be only his tool. I had been leaving him out of the picture. I would not save people; God would. Understanding this was a great relief.

Second, I realized there are many forms of evangelism, and not all people are gifted in the same way. Some are able to speak to total strangers about Jesus in the first five minutes of their meeting and can do so with some success. Others can be effective only when a firm bond of friendship has been established. Still others are most evangelistic through the Christlike quality of their lives. Again, we must go to our prayers so God will use us in accordance with the potentials he has built into us. We can ask him to make of us what he intends for us to be, and we need not worry because we are *not* like someone else. After all, God didn't make everyone a Mozart, or an Einstein, or a Michael Jordan.

Prayers for evangelism have impressive credentials. Jesus told his disciples to pray that God would send laborers into the harvest (Matt. 9:38, to the disciples; Luke 10:2–3, to the seventy). The need was great and the harvest was ripe, he said. This struck me as a wonderful prayer that I could pray. It would reflect my concern for the lost, and would ask God to send "someone" to save them, absolving me from obligation. This bubble was burst by a godly professor who pointed out that God would doubtless send into the harvest those who cared enough about it to pray about it. He suggested the real application of this prayer in a contemporary setting would be, "Lord, send laborers, *and include me in their number."*

Thus we come to God confessing our weaknesses, wanting to be his instruments and part of his great purposes, and praying to that end. The following are some areas to which our prayers might be directed. If they fit, fine. If not, pray about the thing that is your apparent need.

## LOVE

We are called to love all people, and in loving, to want the best for them. If we believe a life with God is part of that best, we may need to wrestle with an apparent gap between our responsibility to love and our resisting the call to evangelism. Is it possible that we do not love people enough? That may be a hard admission, yet if it is true, God already knows it. He awaits our honest recognition of our need so he can begin healing us. If our problem is a lack of an emotional and motivational concern, we know intellectually that God loves the lost, but the knowledge has never become part of our personal concern.

Paul addressed this in 1 Thessalonians 3:12. He told the church he was praying that they would abound in love for one another, and *for all*. In 2 Thessalonians 3:5, Paul repeated this as he asked the Lord to direct the hearts of the Christians in Thessalonica to the love of God. We have previously cited the marvelous prayer in Ephesians 3:17–19. We only remind ourselves here that Paul asked God to deepen both the grasp and the practice of love in the lives of the Ephesians. Would he not do the same for us?

We do not know how God will answer these prayers. What we are urging is that we pray them, with special application to our attitude toward those who do not know Christ. God will respond as he deems best.

## UNDERSTANDING AND INSIGHT

How should we approach people? What should we say to them? Prayer can help us grasp the psychological issues involved in these encounters. It can also strengthen us in the learning and application of the scriptural materials. In our previous discussion of hallowing God's name, we spoke of knowing God. Ephesians 1:17 tells of Paul praying that God would grant a "spirit of wisdom and revelation" in knowing him. In Colossians 1:9, Paul told the church he had prayed that they be filled with the knowledge of God's will "in all spiritual wisdom and understanding." We cannot say how God will answer the prayer for understanding and insight. He may stir within us the desire to study and learn; he may grant us opportunities for service in new communities; he may work in other ways we cannot imagine. We must pray, and God will do his work in meeting our needs.

## WISDOM

We have already cited James 1:5–8 and 3:15–18 and what they say about asking God for wisdom. If we do not know how to go about bearing the message of Christ, then we can turn to God. We must remember, too, that circumstances differ. What is wise in one instance may not be best in another, and we should to pray to be wise in each individual circumstance. I recall the case of a well-meaning friend who so lacked wisdom in his approaches to nonbelievers that in virtually every instance where he introduced the subject (and it was often), he was met with indifference or resentment. There were even those who interpreted his blundering approaches as smacking of unbalanced fanaticism. If we recognize lack of wisdom as our area of need, then, "to our prayers."

## COURAGE AND BOLDNESS

In our survey of Acts, we noted the prohibition leveled against the early Christians by the Jewish Sanhedrin (4:17). They ordered Peter and John not to speak any more in Jesus' name—a frightening mandate, to which disobedience seemed to augur serious consequences. I can empathize with any of the early Christians who might have quailed and wished to retreat from any evangelistic activity. Whatever the psychological condition of the gathered church, they prayed for God to give them boldness in proclamation (4:24–31). And he did! The message continued to sound forth. The courage God planted within the church continued the dramatic spread of Christianity—let the officials do what they might.

As dynamic as Paul was, he may have felt twinges of reticence himself. Whether he did or not, he asked, in Ephesians 6:19, that his fellow Christians would pray for him that he would communicate the mystery of the gospel with boldness.

Personal experience leads me to conclude we may be reluctant to share Christ because we think too much about ourselves and because our Lord is on our minds too little. God may answer our prayers by reversing these mental priorities. He may so infuse us with a sense of his love for us that we become less anxious about any possible rejection we may receive from others. He may so fill us with love for humanity that love will push past all ego-centered barriers.

## THE OPEN DOOR

A text that has had enormous significance in my own life is a prayer in Colossians 4:3–4 Paul asked the church to pray that God would give him an "open door" for the word, so that, though a prisoner, he would declare the "mystery" of Christ "clearly."

Consider: God knows everything there is to know about every person who has ever lived. Of those alive now, he knows their social security numbers, addresses, jobs, incomes, credit card numbers, and innermost thoughts. He knows how they feel about him. And he knows how their moods and beliefs change from day-to-day, even from minute to minute. He knows those who, if approached, would be open to the gospel message.

He knew this about me and sent a person my way whose interest in me led me to be a Christian.

If we pray for the open door, can we not assume that God will give us a connection to these open people, in order to help them discover Christ? Even those people who today are disinterested may have a change of heart tomorrow. Something in their lives may produce a receptivity that formerly was not present. If God would have all men to be saved, and if he intends to use Christians as a prominent means of accomplishing this task, then ought not a constant prayer be for God to open doors into those lives?

Of course, we do not know how this might work. Let us pray and see. We may discover new opportunities. We may make new friendships that prove fruitful. People may come "out of the woodwork" seeking our concern and help. There may even be a case, as with a lawyer friend of mine, when a fellow lawyer came with the direct question, "What must I do to be saved?"

We have addressed "thy kingdom come" primarily in terms of evangelism. As important as this topic is, it has surely left many dimensions of this petition untouched. One of the blessings of continued reflection on this request is the broadened and deepened insight that can come. We are invited to join the quest. In this chapter, we have dealt with two great topics: the call to come to Christ, and the unimaginable power of prayer. Who can say what God may do for Christians who constantly go to him on behalf of those who have not known the blessings of the kingdom? We are challenged to go to our knees, and then rise up to be what God empowers us to be. It may be that our prayers will enable us to be his instruments in making the difference that matters most of all in someone's life.

## Thoughts to Ponder

1. How would you say the kingdom was present in Jesus' ministry?

2. What is meant by "kingdom"?

3. Do you know of conversion stories in which prayer brought the preacher and the convert together?

4. Explain: where God's name is hallowed, there the kingdom has come.

5. How do you react to appeals to practice evangelism?

6. What does your personal inventory of yourself as an evangelist reveal?

7. How do you react to the comments about prayer for the open door?

# Chapter Eight

# Daily Bread

In the request for daily bread, the Lord's Prayer changes from "thy" to "our." But we have already indicated that praying for God's name to be hallowed and for his kingdom to come involves changes within those who pray. Praying for our bread also involves God—the God who provides. Thus the transition from the third person to the first person may not be as drastic as it might seem at first. All three petitions, regardless of the pronouns used, involve both God and man.

Commentators have discussed the seemingly sharp descent from highly spiritual matters to the common—from holiness and kingdom to bread. Because of this startling movement, some have suggested that the bread here may be spiritual bread. Jesus did, after all, identify himself as the bread of life in John 6, and he also indicated that bread, in the Lord's Supper, would symbolize his body.

## Physical Nourishment

I disagree with this "spiritualizing" view. For one thing, it seems to bypass the obvious meaning of the text; for another, it brings repetition, echoing much of what is asked in the other portions of the prayer. But most of all, I resist spiritualizing the meaning of bread here because I think the Lord's Prayer is meant to include the entire scope of human needs. "Hallowed" asks for spiritual enriching. "Kingdom" deals with Christian outreach. The final two petitions, to which we will come later, ask for forgiveness and continuing help in resisting temptation. But humans have material needs, and if they are not addressed in this petition, then where are they addressed?

I believe a survey of Luke's Gospel will strengthen this understanding. When the devil tempted Jesus with food as he starved in the wilderness, Jesus refused this evil attempt to undermine his ministry (Luke 4:3–4). His concerns were of a higher nature. But just because "loaves and fishes" were not his first priority does not mean they were of no importance. No Gospel is as concerned with the plight of the poor or the feeding of the hungry as Luke. And no Gospel shows more abundantly that God will provide for his followers. In 5:1–11, Jesus produced a remarkable catch of fish so that those who "left everything" (v. 11) and followed him knew they would be provided for. Jesus fed five thousand (9:7–9). The twelve (9:1–6) and the seventy (10:1–12) were sent on their missions with the assurance their material needs would be supplied. In the last part of the prayer text in 11:1–13, Jesus used illustrations about food to assure his hearers of God's answer to prayer. Perhaps most directly, in 12:22–34 Jesus told his disciples not to be anxious about food or clothing. "Seek his kingdom, and these things shall be yours as well."

As we consider the prayer for daily bread, then, we will avoid a complete spiritualizing, but we also will avoid making material needs more important than spiritual ones. Nor will we totally dissociate this petition from spiritual concerns, as I hope to show in our continuing discussion.

There is a further assumption I am making about this petition. If the Lord's Prayer does cover the entire span of essential human needs, then I consider the request for daily bread to embrace all needs of the body. Thus we will include in this discussion not only food, but physical safety and security, as well as health. In this last category we will discuss praying for the sick, surely one of the most practical but also most perplexing aspects of Christian prayer.

But first, let us discuss literal food. Though it may not change the larger sense of the prayer, the word "daily" has perplexed students for many years. The Greek word is found in Scripture only here and in Matthew's parallel (Matt. 6:11). Nor has it been found in any Greek writing for several centuries before or after the writing of the New Testament. Consequently, there are no literary contexts to help us in determining its meaning. Much has been written on the subject, and Luke Timothy Johnson has summed up the discussion by noting that three basic theories have emerged. Some consider it to mean "daily" in the obvious sense—that is, today and each day. Others hold that "bread for the morrow," as a soldier's rations, is the best understanding. The third conjecture is that the request is for one's "necessary" bread. There are great truths to obtain in each of these cases.

One matter that Luke stresses repeatedly is the folly of trusting material wealth for security. For example, he introduces us to several rich men whose misplaced trust spelled disaster. The "rich fool" (12:13–22) ignored the need to prepare for death; the rich man at whose gate Lazarus died made the same tragic error (16:19–31). The rich ruler could not release the "security" of his riches for the greater security of treasure in heaven (18:23–24). The theme of these stories is woven throughout the rest of Luke's narrative. It is God to whom ultimate trust must be given. The prayer for daily bread recognizes that regardless of one's material status, the disciple sees God as the source of all that exists and the only one upon whom sure reliance for the needs of life can be placed, not income, or inheritance, or investments, or retirement provisions, or government subsidies. To rely on these and not on God is the great folly. Even if other circumstances seem to promise that one would be provided for regardless of what might come, this prayer still recognizes the truth about the real Provider, who is God!

Thus this petition is a cure for the greed that so saturates our country. We want more and more, beyond our needs and even beyond the possibility of our use. We are trained to want. In addition, we are so insecure and worried about the future that we surround ourselves with all manner of material safety devices against possible future danger. Certainly any one should use good sense in providing for the days to come, but the Christian realizes the best provision of all is to seek first God's kingdom. "Give us each day our daily bread" is not only a request, but a reminder that can effect inner transformation as we pray it.

Whatever the precise meaning of the word "daily," when we pray this word we are making a continual affirmation of trust in God. When Jesus spoke of bearing the cross "daily" (Luke 9:32), he indicated that discipleship is to be affirmed again and again. Both in cross-bearing and in depending on God for bread, there is no way to make one great commitment for life and then to forget it as the days go by. Each day, trust must be renewed. This is done on days that begin and end exuberantly and on those that begin and end dismally. In effect, every day the Christian says to God, "I acknowledge my need and appeal to your love and power to provide for me."

The result of making this petition and receiving God's answer is to produce a sense of gratitude—a commodity that for many people is in short supply. The more fully we recognize our real dependence and his gracious provision, the more gratitude will move to center stage in our lives. And gratitude is the great motivator: the stronger its presence, the more fervor will characterize our discipleship.

Prayer is not a guarantee bread will be given—we must recognize the many people who lack their basic needs, as well as those who have been miraculously rescued from dire circumstances. But the central point here is a recognition of the source of food. All bread ever produced has been made, ultimately, by God. Thus Jesus is calling his followers, as they receive food, to recognize its true source.

## Physical Safety

Let us now consider prayers for physical safety. These come from three sources. First is a warning by Jesus himself; second is a series of texts from Paul's writings; and third is a reference from John.

In Mark 13:18 (see also Matt. 24:20), Jesus warned his disciples about the coming destruction of Jerusalem. "Pray that it may not happen in winter" were his words. Matthew reports the same message, with the additional "or on the Sabbath." These are accompanied by special concerns for pregnant women, or women with children. It would be a terrible time—a prediction confirmed by the postdestruction testimony of the Jewish historian Josephus. It is hard to know if Jesus was placing the focus here on the power of prayer, or on the horrors of the devastation to come. Whatever the case, when the city fell in AD 70 and those Christians who escaped the city fled to Pella, it was in the latter part of the summer (our July–September). Thus the fugitives did not have to endure the rigors of inclement weather when they fled.

Now let us consider the citations from Paul. In 2 Thessalonians 3:2, Romans 15:31, 2 Corinthians 1:11, and many others, Paul besought the

Christians to pray that he might be delivered from wicked and evil men. It might appear that the apostle was concerned most of all for his personal safety, but reflection shows his concern for safety was insignificant compared to his greater concern for the spread of the gospel. When considering Paul's total career, one sees clearly that personal safety was not his central concern. It was his evangelistic endeavors that he did not want blocked. The suggestion here for Christians of all ages is that their prayers center in asking for opportunities for conveying God's message.

In fact, the New Testament as a whole seems concerned not so much about the personal physical safety of Christians as it is for their spiritual welfare and the spread of the gospel. We know that Jesus seemed heedless of personal safety as he completed his mission. The early Christians defied the authorities—not a safe thing—when told to speak no more in Jesus' name. Paul was certainly not prudent regarding his physical welfare as he pressed on in his ministry. We do recall that Jesus spoke of cross-bearing, which he modeled powerfully and conveyed a frightening sense of "reckless abandon" in making the pilgrimage.

Now let me cite a common prayer that can stand for a class of prayers. Often Christians pray that God will keep them safe as they travel. I recall the first time I took an auto trip that began with the owner of the car praying for safe travel. At first I was impressed, but my perspective later reversed as he drove eighty miles per hour, at night and in the fog, on a winding two lane road. His prayer, I later thought, was for God to save a fool from his own folly. Since then I have been reluctant about such prayers, preferring to pray something like, "Lord, help me to drive carefully, alert to possible problems, like a sane man." Even when we have prayed such a prayer and benefitted from the answer, there are dangers from others that our best efforts cannot deter. A motorist suddenly pulls from a side road directly into our path. The driver of the car approaching us at a high speed loses control and hits us head on. A drunk driver causes a terrible, unavoidable accident.

We want to be safe. We do not want to be hurt. We want our bodies to remain whole. Because these concerns are "so much with us" we invariably pray about them. But—as best I see it—this kind of personal preservation isn't what Christians were praying for in the New Testament nor what we are instructed to pray for. We might ask ourselves in this regard, is our view of prayer truly biblical and truly Christian, or is it somewhat self-centered? Facing this difficult question honestly may resolve some of our difficulties about prayer.

Recall Paul's "thorn in the flesh" (2 Cor. 12:6–10). This burden, whatever its nature, was so onerous Paul begged the Lord three times to remove it. His concern is understandable. But God's concern was not merely to alleviate the problem. The divine response allowed the thorn to remain but coupled it with a great blessing, assuring Paul, "My grace is sufficient for you." The result was that God's power was "made perfect in weakness." Paul, asking for the lesser relief (which we are inclined to think is all-important), was given a gift of larger import. So, again, the text shows that God's primary concern was not freedom from pain. He may even bestow pain (or allow it to be bestowed), if in so doing his work can be enhanced (cf. Heb. 12:1–11). This is a hard lesson for the church to learn in an age where "feeling good" is so important, and where some even make it the center of the Christian faith. We want so much to be comfortable. But as we have noted before, and as Paul seems to have realized, the request before and beneath all prayers should be, "thy will be done."

In the United States, where the practice of Christianity is generally pursued by those who are ensconced in a certain degree of comfort, circumstances similar to those faced by Paul seem foreign. Yet even here, and certainly in many other parts of the world, a prayer for physical safety for the kingdom's sake may be an urgent need. Those who are aware of the dangers posed in many mission contexts around the world could certainly supply enough illustrations to this point.

## Physical Healing

Our last section under "daily bread" concerns prayer for the sick. This is one of the hardest issues I have had to address, not because determining the scriptural teaching is difficult, but because it is so unpopular, and against the emphases of so much prayer. It is difficult also because what is to be said may seem callous and unkind. But this apparent coldness does not represent my heart. C. S. Lewis says in *The Problem of Pain* that he asked himself how he could speak to his readers with sufficient tenderness when making a point that might seem to them hard and heartless. I find myself in the same position.

Let us work our way into this discussion by noting contemporary Christian custom, and then by surveying some problems. In my world, and likely in yours, a time of corporate prayer is often preceded by prayer requests, which are almost exclusively offered for those who are sick or in physical distress. In the university where I teach, we hold a daily chapel service for the entire university community. During this time, announcements are made of prayer needs—a matter taken most seriously by the student body. Here most of the requests deal with some aspect of physical well-being. Prayer lists in church bulletins and oral requests in church meetings are of the same sort. A stranger unacquainted with Christian faith and customs could easily conclude from observation that such prayer constituted the greatest interest of our prayer lives.

It might seem villainous to challenge this emphasis, but many thinking Christians have voiced problems with this overwhelming concern:

1—All of us can point to instances where we are convinced that prayer has brought healing. As I write now, I think of a talented Christian brother whose life was threatened by a severe form of cancer and who called many Christian friends to enter with him into a covenant of prayer. Since his last siege with the disease, he has enjoyed over two decades cancer-free. These years have seen him engaged in significant ministry. It is our conviction that God has responded to the prayers for his healing.

But we also know of many other cases where earnest prayer has been made for the sick, but they have not survived. I can recall more than one instance where there has been damage to the personal faith of those whose prayers for healing were not answered. Believing wrongly that God promised to answer any prayer made in faith, they argue that they did pray in faith but that God's did not honor his promise. The fact is that the sick do *not* always recover, no matter how frequent and how fervent the prayers on their behalf. Why does God heal some and not others? I know of no human wisdom great enough to answer this dilemma. Some may give glib and shallow formulae, but the ultimate truth lies hidden from human hearts.

2—God knows about even the smallest details of our lives. But can we believe that he determines to remove all human suffering in this life? From our previous discussion, it would appear not, since Jesus and many of his followers have suffered persecution and even martyrdom. A view of prayer that says sickness is something contrary to God's rule, and that it is a thing he would not allow, runs aground on the rocks of human experience and Scripture. Physical wellness, no matter how devoutly desired, apparently is not guaranteed by God, pray as we will.

3—All theologies of prayer for health must come up against the barrier of death. Physical death, to Christians, is not the great enemy but is rather the doorway to greater glory. We must all die. But what if our prayers are denying that reality by pushing death away? Do we think that if we keep praying we will exist forever in these frail bodies? Are we asking God to reverse the universal destiny of humankind? Is it possible that some views of prayer for the sick represent a philosophy that is contradictory to the Christian view of death and resurrection? Pain, though sometimes excruciating, may be a source of great blessing. It reveals needs, even other than the physical, that must be attended to, and it gives the opportunity for the powerful building of Christian character.

Our prayers may not be for the indefinite extension of life, but only that death come at the appropriate time. But since the age at death is not identical for all humans, who can know what that time is? We may say that a young death leaves opportunities unmet. True, but we have faith in opportunities beyond this physical life. And to Christians, death at whatever age is a triumph, not a defeat.

4—This brings us to the last problem, one I approach with fear and trembling. I hope nothing said here will be understood as minimizing the grief people feel or as being insensitive to those in sorrow. But we must face the truth. Often, our prayers for the sick are more for us than for them. To put it bluntly, such prayers have a large measure of self-interest. We do not wish others to suffer, but certainly we do not want to suffer because of them— even because we might lose them. I do not think this is the argument to use in all cases. But when our passions fade and we can analyze our reactions, we usually know whether we were praying as much for ourselves as we were for the person afflicted or departed. I am not condemning this quite natural reaction, but we must consider the point as we think about prayers and health.

Since we recognize that several problems confront our prayers for the sick, why do such prayers loom so large in our prayer lives? It is because we are so concerned when we or those we love are faced with serious illness or injury. It is only natural that we carry our concerns to the Highest Power. But these concerns draw further impetus from the healing activities of Jesus and the early Christians. All readers of the Gospels know how often Jesus healed, but only a few of these references couple the healing with prayer. Here are a few references where prayer and healing are coupled in the Gospels as well as in the rest of the New Testament.

1–Mark 7:34. A deaf man with a speech impediment was brought to Jesus, who took him aside and after some further activity restored both his speech and hearing. In the process, Jesus looked to heaven, sighed, and said to the man, "be opened."

2–Mark 9:29. On his return from the Mount of Transfiguration, Jesus healed a demoniac whom the demon had plagued with epilepsy. Certain disciples, when previously approached, had been unable to heal the unfortunate boy. After the healing, they asked Jesus why they had failed. His answer was, "This kind cannot be driven out by anything but prayer."

3–John 11:41–44. This is the famous story of the raising of Lazarus from the dead. The tomb was opened, and Jesus prayed, thanking God for hearing him (praying for Lazarus?). Then, in one of Scripture's most dramatic scenes, Lazarus, bound with grave clothes, emerged from the tomb.

I want to add here a brief word about the healings of Jesus. It was not his primary concern to make the sick well. If it had been, all the sick would have been healed, and, by extension, no one would ever die. The healings, I believe, demonstrated his power and also marked God as a God of compassion. They pointed to the greater healing, salvation from sin, and to the greater victory over death, beyond the cessation of physical existence.

4–Acts 4:30. This prayer follows the "official" Jewish prohibition of speaking or teaching in Jesus' name. The response of the church was to appeal to a higher court; to God. They asked God to grant them boldness in preaching, as well as to stretch out his hand to heal and perform signs and wonders through the name of Jesus. Verse 31 says God answered the prayer and they did speak the Word of God with boldness. Signs and wonders—healings—are next mentioned in Acts 5:12-16. The point of these wonders was to enhance the teaching of the church and lead to conversions. There could be no doubt, under such circumstances, that God was with them. One gets the impression that the healings of the body, marvelous as they were, were intended to point to healing of the soul—forgiveness.

5–Acts 9:40. The godly widow, Dorcas, was brought back from the dead when Peter prayed and said, "Tabitha, rise"—another event testifying to the great power of God brought to bear in human events through prayer.

6–2 Corinthians 12:6–10. Paul's prayer for healing from the messenger of Satan, the mysterious "thorn in the flesh," was not granted. Instead, he was given a greater blessing—strength out of weakness.

7–James 5:13–18. We read:

> Is any one among you suffering? Let him pray. Is any cheerful? Let him sing praise. Is any among you sick? Let him call for the elders of the church, and let them pray over him, anointing him with oil in the name of the Lord; and the prayer of faith will save the sick man, and the Lord will raise him up; and if he has committed sins, he will be forgiven. Therefore confess your sins to one another, and pray for one another, that you may be healed. The prayer of a righteous man has great power in its effects. Elijah was a man of like nature with ourselves and he prayed fervently that it might not rain, and for three years and six months it did not rain on the earth. Then he prayed again and the heaven gave rain, and the earth brought forth its fruit.

This is the only New Testament text that instructs Christians to pray for the sick. The other texts just considered speak of supernatural healings, but give no instructions to the church about praying, either in the first century or today. Thus, the importance of James 5 looms large.

Since this last passage is so central, let us analyze it further. The prayer for the sick is not the only prayer in the context. There were also the prayer in suffering and the praise (a type of prayer) by those who were cheerful (v. 13). In addition to the prayer of the elders for the sick man, there were the prayers of those in the community for one another (v. 16). Finally, there were the prayers of Elijah (cf. 1 Kings 17, 18) in the history of North Israel (v. 17–18).

The larger context into which all this is set was an encouragement to a suffering church. Chapter 1:2 speaks of meeting "various trials," and the last two verses of the book speak of bringing a sinner back from the "error of his way." This latter phrase may assume trials that would have the effect of drawing people away from God. In the same vein see 1:12; 2:6–7, and 5:1–11. Thus the suffering in 5:13 may have been experienced by Christians because of opposition to their faith. The reference to cheerfulness may speak of those who were not defeated by their trials.

Ralph Martin reminds us that, within the text of James, some prayers fail (4:1–3) and some succeed (1:5, 6). The motive of the one praying was of crucial importance. Above all, no interpretation of prayer for healing should fail to consider the wider purposes of God. Further, Martin writes, this text issues a call to spiritual wholeness, in which sins are forgiven, not just to physical well-being. God's purposes are broader than healing of the body, and we who pray must keep this in mind. It is possible to place such a strong emphasis on physical healing that one's whole concept of Christianity becomes skewed.

What are we to conclude from all this about personal belief and practice? The text teaches the importance of patience and trust in adversity, and also shows the importance of prayer in times of gladness, or sickness, or sinfulness. It indicates a prayer responsibility involving the whole Christian community, and in that connection speaks of the importance of confession.

When one surveys the total scope of James 5:13–18, prayer for the sick, though of significance, is reduced from the absolute center of the text. So how are Christians to pray for the sick? Pray we will. The situations we encounter are too immediate and demanding to let us do otherwise. Love and compassion impel us. They would lead us to carry concerns to God even if we had no instruction in this regard. And the sick are sometimes healed, as both experience and Scripture testify. Thus, I offer the following suggestions.

1. We can pray for the sick even though there is much we do not understand. As indicated before, we are called to faith, not necessarily to comprehension.

2. Let us pray that the sick will glorify God in their illness. Christian history is replete with cases where the Christlike demeanor of the gravely ill has borne mighty witness to God's power in a life. On occasion, even those in the direct terminal circumstances have shown sweet and surrendered spirits that proclaimed God's presence. A Christian neighbor who suffers from terminal cancer has been a source of great inspiration to my wife and me because of the way her faith has achieved greater luster in her final days. She speaks in glowing terms of the hope of heaven that awaits her.

3. Let us pray that, if possible, the ill can grow through their suffering. We again recall the threefold cry of the apostle for the thorn to be removed, and yet his suffering was not relieved. Rather he learned how God's strength was made perfect through weakness.

Praying for the sick is important because it is a healthy expression of compassion. If nothing else were involved, this alone would be a significant Christian action, and one that reflects God's compassion for us.

In crisis circumstances, requests are often sent out to believers asking them to join in prayer for the person or cause at issue. There seems to be an assumption that many prayers are more powerful than few. It is certainly good to have many people in a caring and concerned relation to the matter under consideration. But, scripturally, it is hard to discover guidance on this issue. Isn't one petition to the Father of great power?

Can God really be overwhelmed or persuaded by many requests? Thinking Christians would not agree to this. But we still call many hearts to join in prayer, and it seems appropriate that we do so. Paul did the same (see Rom. 15:31; 2 Cor. 1:11; Phil. 1:19). Here is another practice in which we engage without fully understanding what happens. Without knowing how, we assume quantity and fervency of prayer does make a difference.

## Thoughts to Ponder

1. How do you deal with the issue of starving Christians who do not have daily bread, despite their prayers?

2. Why do we pray for rulers? What if they are evil, with no interest in helping their subjects to live a "quiet and godly life"?

3. How do you feel about praying for a safe trip?

4. Why does God not heal every sick Christian for whom prayer is made?

# CHAPTER NINE

# FORGIVE OUR SINS

If our greatest physical need is daily bread, one of our greatest spiritual needs is to have our sins forgiven. We have argued that the first two petitions, centering in God's name and his kingdom, are fulfilled, in part, as he empowers humans to glorify him and live out his kingdom. But we have assumed God will work in these ways in a redeemed life, and a redeemed life has been rescued from its state of enmity to God, that is, has had its sins forgiven. Thus, we can see the imperative need for forgiveness.

The dread power of sin was treated with utmost seriousness by Jesus. Without forgiveness one continues in the self-centered grip of satanic power. Yet the desperate human plight is that no unaided human effort can produce a life free of sin, nor can it charge the gates of heaven and compel God to bestow forgiveness. The situation is hopeless unless there should be some great act of divine mercy. That act of God is the heart of the gospel story. It is grace, written large, throughout the pages of Scripture.

If mercy did not exist, then there would be no reconciliation with God. And if no reconciliation was offered, there would be no hope of ultimate fellowship with the Maker. A religion that does not offer forgiveness bypasses the most basic human problem. Such a religion may give a heartwarming, visceral sense of the transcendent, or it may satisfy humankind's religious urges, but it still leaves each fallible human caught in a web of hopelessness.

The terrible nature of sin cannot be minimized—as many in all ages have attempted to do. On the other hand, neither can grace be minimized, or the cross and resurrection are emptied of their power.

There are two aspects of this issue: God's great love for sinners, a love that claims and refreshes sinful lives, and the continual dealing with the sin problem within the shelter of life in Christ. The Lord's Prayer is dealing with the second of these, but our appreciation of the matter can be enhanced by a look at the first. Luke's Gospel powerfully demonstrates this theme of God's love for sinners.

## GOD'S LOVE FOR SINNERS

Luke introduces us to a number of "sinners," some of whom are mentioned only by him. Though Jesus spoke with decisive power about the greed and hypocrisy of many in his day, he was compassionate to those who recognized their sinful state and could be attracted to a new way of life. Both the Gospel and Acts are filled with inspiring stories about changed lives. We recall Simon Peter, whose call to follow Jesus came only after Peter besought Jesus to leave him, "for I am a sinful man" (5:11). Luke 7:36–50 tells of the sinful woman in the house of Simon the Pharisee who received forgiveness of sins (in spite of Simon's scorn for her). The confession of the thief on the cross who confirmed both his own wickedness and his faith in Jesus and who was promised a place in Paradise is unique to Luke (23:41–43). The high significance of forgiveness is shown in the case of the paralytic lowered through the roof, to whom Jesus granted forgiveness, and whom he healed as a sign that he could heal the spirit as well as the body (5:17–26). The word for "sins" is found in Luke 3:3; 5:20, 21, 23, 24; 7:47–49; 11:4; and 24:47, and in and each of these instances, forgiveness is offered.

The book of Acts is a story of conversions, each of which depicts God's mercy for sinners. Among many cases, we note mercy even for those who crucified the Lord and Christ (2:36–41). One of the key events in the early church was the conversion of Saul of Tarsus, who had been a potent force in a terrible persecution of Jerusalem Christians (9:1–19). Saul, who became Paul, marveled in his later Christian writings at the love of a God who could forgive his terrible wrongs (cf. 1 Tim. 1:12–17).

Further indication of the powerful way Luke presents God's love for sinners is found in the language he uses. The Greek term translated "forgiveness" is found seventeen times in the New Testament, and ten of these are in Luke and Acts. Luke 1:77 and 3:3 are connected with John's preaching of forgiveness, granted upon confession of sins and baptism. Luke 24:47 is the commission to the apostles to preach repentance and remission of sins. They would do this once they were empowered by the Spirit that the resurrected Lord would pour out on them. The term is used twice in Luke 4:18, first translated "release" and then, "go free" (NRSV). In both these instances, one could easily conclude that forgiveness of sins was the meaning.

In Acts 2:38, forgiveness was the promise of the new age given to repentant believers who submitted to baptism. In Acts 5:31, Peter and the apostles, standing defiantly before the Jewish high council, announced that God had raised Jesus in order to "give repentance to Israel and forgiveness of sins." Peter's sermon to the household of Cornelius in Acts 10:43 said every one who believed in him would receive forgiveness of sins through his name. A similar word was preached by Paul in the synagogue at Antioch (13:38). Finally, as Paul repeated his conversion story in Acts 26:18, he echoed Jesus' commission that he should preach to the Gentiles that "they might receive forgiveness of sins."

From all this, we note the earnestness with which Jesus and Luke addressed this issue.

Jesus, the God-man, was bringing to earth a new way of reconciliation with God. Forgiveness for the Israelites was associated with the annual Day of Atonement and its ritual (Lev. 16), as well as with the various sacrifices for "unwitting" sins (Lev. 1–7). There were also prayers for God's forgiveness, as evidenced, for example, by the passionate cries of Psalm 51:1–2, 7, and 9. But all of this activity sprang from within the context of God's covenant relation to Israel. Now Jesus offered forgiveness apart from these rituals, as a direct gift of God, upon the ground of faith. Jews who heard Jesus' prayer instructions would recognize they were moving into a new way of relating to God.

Luke probably wrote his Gospel for Gentile Christians, and in the Gentile world the attitude toward sin was different. Though that world was excessively sinful (even granting that Paul may have made the case seem as dreadful as possible in Rom. 1:18–32), there was not a sense that sin was a thing that clung to people, or that one's past evils had to be taken away to be right with any deity. Rather, the prevailing sense was that to be right one simply had to begin doing the right things. For Gentiles, then, Jesus' teaching about forgiveness indicated a different view of human need than the commonly accepted perspective.

## Forgiveness in the Church

We have been speaking of sin as the cleansing of the "alien sinner." The Lord's Prayer, however, was given to disciples, so we now move to consider the place of forgiveness within the church. Though Jesus could speak God's word of forgiveness however he wished during his earthly sojourn, this continuing blessing through the following years depended on his death and resurrection. Luke's readers knew that was true, though those who had heard Jesus would not have grasped then just how this forgiveness would be made possible. In other words, Jesus' words were a sort of prediction about what was to be accomplished as his ministry reached its full intent. Recall that Jesus, nailed to the cross, cried "Father, forgive them" (Luke 23:34). It was in that very death and the subsequent conquest of death that his words were made possible. He prayed even for his torturers—who can grasp the wonder of it?

It is a wonder to be born again, to be forgiven. But temptation remains, and for humans the need for forgiveness is a lifelong need. Christianity provides not only the initial purification but also the promise of continual cleansing through the once-for-all sacrifice of Jesus. However, that cleansing must be sought by continued exhibitions of faith—hence, "forgive us of our sins." To have been cleansed once with no promise of further purification would not solve the deadly sin problem. Christians, knowing their inner selves and the "demons" that beset them, gratefully receive the promise enshrined in this petition. When any of us reflects on what we are in our own hearts—even the best of us—we are amazed at the love and patience of our Lord. We have failed so often, but the list of our transgressions is never longer than the offer of his forgiving grace. We remember Simon the sorcerer, who tried to buy the power to control God's Spirit. Peter's harsh condemnation consigned him to perdition.

But even then the possibility of forgiveness was open, if he would repent and pray, as we see in Acts 8:9–24.

Once, many years ago, I was preaching an evangelistic series in a small town. In attendance at the service was a godly leader from a church in a nearby city. He was asked to lead prayer, and did so, wording an exceptional petition. Later, after church, he reflected on his prayer with the comment, "I left out the most important thing." "What was that?" "I forgot to ask for forgiveness," he replied.

I have often reflected on this episode. Of course, our prayers do not earn God's forgiveness. Surely God knows our needs even when they do not come to our lips. The Spirit, we remember, carries the things deep within us to the Father (Rom. 8:26). Yet the temptation is to minimize our sin and act as if forgiveness is automatic. But to hold this attitude is to ignore our hearts and our needs. The brother was right. "Forgiveness" is one of the most important prayers we can pray, and thanks to God who makes this possible. We should never neglect it.

Forgiving sins was such a radical act of Jesus that he was criticized for it (Luke 5:21; 7:49). Of course, many of his contemporaries expressed indignation at what they perceived to be Jesus' usurping the prerogatives of God. But that indignation would not have been so great had the gift not been so basic and so magnificent. Jesus was not trifling with a peripheral religious issue. He was aiming at the center of the human relation to God.

The previous petition of the Lord's Prayer for daily bread asked for what was necessary to live. Forgiveness, though, is necessary for one to die. This promise carries with it the history of an entire life. As often as we sin (and how often that is) we need forgiveness. We probably cannot go a single hour (or minute?) without sinning, without wanting to displace God with self. In praying, "Forgive us our sins," we express our desire to grow and to have greater insight into both self and God.

We spoke above of God's mercy and patience. We can observe this reality theologically, but more of its wonder comes home to me when I see it personally. I reflect on the half century I have been a Christian and shudder as I recall the number of misdeeds in thought, action, and omissions that have spotted my life. So many of them are the same failures over and over. I think, too, of how often I have asked God to forgive again today what I had asked him to forgive yesterday. Sometimes there seems to be no improvement at all; sometimes there even seems to be retrogression. Yet there stands that promise, that prayer, and that God. Once more, God gives healing. How can he be so patient, so long-suffering with my sins? The wonder of it is beyond calculation. If ever there was a reason for humility and thanksgiving, it is here.

How can the power of this prayer impact us more fully? There have been times when Christians were inclined to be oversensitive to their sins, and their Christianity was characterized by a fearful expectation of judgment. This was unhealthy, but today we may have shifted to an opposite extreme. We naively assume that humans are basically good—a view that the Bible clearly contradicts. Or we minimize sin by substituting a milder vocabulary for the terrible reality. We use words like mistakes, or miscalculations, or errors in judgment, or inconsistencies. We may, like the first couple in Scripture and like millions of their descendants, deny the truth by diverting blame from ourselves to another person, or set of circumstances, or even to God himself (see Gen. 3:12).

So we need to come face to face with the truth and quit fooling ourselves. We are sinners—horrors to God and ourselves if the truth be known—and we can only be cured when we admit our illness. It is said an alcoholic can be set on the road to sobriety only upon admission of the addictive problem. So with sin. "My name is Tony, and I am a sinner." And so say we all. But this prayer allows us to add, "I have been forgiven by God's love and grace, made potent by Jesus' death and burial and my union with that great gift of God."

Not only do we need to make the admission, we need to recognize both the basic sin that infects us, and the sins that flow from it. We are self-centered, and we will, with the slightest nudge, shove God and others out of the way to get what we want. God's forgiveness sets us on the path of service and self-sacrifice in which we hold God as our first priority and we consider others better than ourselves. Then, as we see this and say our prayers for forgiveness, we come to a more insightful grasp of the specific sins that characterize us, positively and negatively, in thought, word, and action. As these surface, God's power can address them as we acknowledge and confess them. The obvious flaws become subjects of prayer, as do the hidden transgressions that may be the more serious because they are concealed. Thus, the prayer for forgiveness not only appeals for cleansing, but also affords opportunity for growth into the image of Christ.

Recall that there are also New Testament texts instructing Christians to intercede for one another, asking God to forgive others. Stephen, as his Lord had done, prayed that God would not hold their sin against his killers. As we have already recognized, Luke was deliberately paralleling the death of this first martyr with the death of his Master, and the comparison leads us to believe that God's mercy was granted even to such as took Stephen's life. With the introduction of Saul at this point in the story, we witness a glorious answer to Stephen's prayer.

And again, Simon, when scored for his attempt to measure God's Spirit with money, begged Peter to pray for him (Acts 8:22). This request shows how deeply he was struck with the wrong he had done, and how eager he was to again be right with God. Beyond this, James 5:15–16 speaks of praying for one another as sins are confessed, and 1 John 5:16 instructs the readers to pray for a Christian brother.

We have maintained throughout these pages that in praying for others, we should not ask God to violate their free will. If others choose to sin, and have no inclination to repent, then any prayer for forgiveness would be useless. Yet there are still many ways we can pray in such cases, especially that God may give us wisdom and opportunity to lovingly bring an errant Christian to repentance and forgiveness. In a later chapter, we will discuss prayers of intercession and will meet these ideas again.

When God promises to grant forgiveness and Christians respond to that promise, it is important to recognize that God *does* forgive. Though the cry for forgiveness may or may not be accompanied with deep emotion, God's answer does not depend on one's feelings or intensity of petition. Sometimes we mistakenly make this connection. Thus we may feel our prayer has not been adequate, or that an answer has not come. After all, forgiveness is a thing that takes place in the heart of God, not in our emotions. Yet we should certainly sense relief knowing that God honors his promise.

Unfortunately, some Christians still bear damaging inner burdens that they need not bear. When God has cleansed us, we are free from sin. But it is not uncommon for feelings of guilt to remain when they should be released. Often we cannot go back and undo the wrongs we have done.

We fret because we did not treat a relative properly before he or she died, or because of misdeeds that led to a broken marriage, or because we failed as parents, or as children. Everyone has a list of severe regrets. The glory of Christianity is that though we feel deep sorrow, the dominant realization is relief that we have been freed. We are out of prison. Let us rejoice in that freedom!

## FORGIVING EACH OTHER

The symmetry of this prayer is interrupted by the next phrase, "for we ourselves forgive every one who is indebted to us." Since the rest of the passage (11:2–4) gives instructions regarding what to request, this departure from the form must be deemed highly significant. The prayer for forgiveness of one's own sins is nullified in the life of the unforgiving disciple. But the implementation of this word can be exceedingly difficult. Sometimes all that can be done is to ask God for the power to begin even wanting to forgive others. How can a rape victim forgive her attacker? How can those tortured in wartime forgive their torturers? How can the elderly person who has been bilked out of all he or she possesses forgive the person who took advantage of him or her? Simple obedience to this word is complicated by the intense emotions that rise when one has been victimized—not to mention lesser indignities and irritations.

Yet here the statement stands, squarely in the middle of the Gospel, and there is no hint it can be bypassed. It is God's message, and those who submit to God are called to submission here. Forgiveness reflects the very nature of God, and the refusal to forgive is a refusal to model one's life after the divine nature. Jesus was no idealist, spouting lofty-sounding moral instructions that he would not keep when the pressure was on him. While tortured on the cross, having been nailed there after a grueling series of indignities, his prayer was, "Father, forgive them" (Luke 23:34). His teaching was underlined and highlighted by his practice. When this call to forgive seems more than we can bear, we remember the Lord. To forgive others lies at the very heart of the faith and cannot be denied without a denial of the very nature and purpose of God.

Because this is such a challenging commission, and so often contrary to one's feelings, we look for ways to circumvent it. One such dodge says we are not obligated to forgive if the offender has not asked our forgiveness or offered an apology. Another is to argue that forgiveness can be denied if the wrongdoer has not repented. Others argue that a point comes, after forgiveness has been offered repeatedly, when the offended party says they will withhold forgiveness until there is a change of behavior. To use a trivial example, a harried wife who has picked up after her husband for years, receives yet another apology for socks dumped on the bedroom floor. In her frustration, she tells her husband that she has no more interest in forgiveness, but in *change*.

In all of this, however, not one of these excuses, or any other, can be used to justify the absence of a willingness to forgive. Whether or not there is remorse, or apology, or recognition of wrong done, or an authentic acceptance of forgiveness, the forgiving spirit is standard equipment for Christians, and we should always be ready to share it, whatever the situation.

Volumes could be written on this subject. But for the present purposes we remember that Jesus' instruction in prayer asks us to cry out in our need, but he also warns us that prayer should come from a life that makes a concerted effort to live according to the mind of Christ. Throughout history there are powerful stories of those who have lived this way in spite of crushing wrongs done to them. Stephen, noted above, is a showcase example—it has been said that if Stephen had not so prayed, Paul would not have so preached.

### Thoughts to Ponder

1. How dare we ask to have our sins forgiven?

2. How does today's culture tend to minimize the reality of sin?

3. How can we deal with the fact that sins are forgiven by God, but emotionally we do not feel forgiven?

# CHAPTER TEN

# LEAD US NOT INTO TEMPTATION

Believers the world over have been repeating the Lord's Prayer since the beginning of Christianity. But with regard to the last petition, "lead us not into temptation," we might well ask if those who pray know exactly what they are asking of God. The easiest way to determine the nature of this request is to look at the additional clause in Matthew 6:19, "but deliver us from evil." If we assume that this is a restatement of the previous line in different language, then the prayer would be for God to keep his people from being overcome by temptation. This fits neatly with the view that sees the complete Lord's Prayer as covering all aspects of the Christian life.

"Hallowed be thy name" is the prayer for personal holiness.
"Thy kingdom come" is the prayer for outreach.
"Give us this day our daily bread" is the prayer for physical needs.
"Forgive us our sins" is the prayer for sins to be forgiven.
"Lead us not into temptation" is the prayer for strength in overcoming temptation.

Still, this apparent simplicity can cover some interpretive problems. Let me illustrate by citing a question I have often heard when teaching about this last petition. "Do these words mean that if we don't pray God *will* lead us into temptation?" Of course they don't. James 1:13–14 clearly indicates

121

that God does not tempt, but James 1:2 also speaks of trials and describes this world as one in which God allows people, even his own people, to experience difficulty. However, the question does show the text is not as simple as it appears at first glance. For example, what is meant by the word translated "temptation"? What is the significance of "evil" in the longer account in Matthew 6:13? If we examine these matters and still come out with the simple answers with which we entered, it has nonetheless been worth while to strive to understand what Scripture is saying.

John Nolland, in his outstanding commentary on Luke, describes three questions posed by the text. First, does God test or tempt? Second, does the temptation or trial in the text refer to the crises of the end time? Third, should we ask to be spared trials or temptations when they are an inevitable part of life?

We have already given attention to the first question. James 1:2–4 speaks of the strengthening value of life's trials. They are to be met with joy, for they can create a steadfastness that leads to a mature faith. We do not need Scripture to inform us that life brings trials, but we need God to give us the resources to turn them from liabilities to assets, for there is a difference between the trials that can improve us and the temptations that can destroy us. James 1:13 says, "God cannot be tempted with evil, and he himself tempts no one," making it clear that God, who would redeem us, will not contradict himself by enticing us to do evil.

With regard to Nolland's second and third issues, to what temptation or trial does the text refer? The Greek term can be rendered either "temptation" or "trial," and the English versions differ in translation. Some argue that the trials are crises that will come at the end time, but this view seems foreign to the intents of Jesus and to the concerns of Luke as he records this instruction. Life is full of trials, and they cannot be escaped, no matter how much we might wish it or how frequent and fervent our prayers.

Alternately, if we read the terms as "temptations," we find still more questions: Is it appropriate for believers to ask to be delivered from all temptation? How could we choose to resist temptation if all temptations had been removed? What would be the point of giving us the power to choose whether to resist temptation or to succumb to it? Jesus said "temptations to sin are sure to come" (Luke 17:1). They cannot be avoided. Jesus does *not* say that through prayer God will deliver us into a temptation-free zone. Even if no temptations came from outside us, there would still be those generated within our fallen natures, especially by our tendency toward self-centeredness.

There is a wide consensus among students of this text that Jesus referred to unusual pressures and trials that were of such a severity they could lead to a denial of the faith. This would mean, as one author put it, that the prayer asks, "Don't let us get in where the water is over our heads and we can't swim." This interpretation allows for the human situation as we know it while also allowing for God's powerful response to prayer. Of course, the exact "stuff" of this prayer will differ from person to person. For one, it might be asking for help in avoiding a situation where sexual temptations would be too hard to resist. Another might request God's aid in avoiding companionships that could lead away from God. Yet another might plead for escape from the need for attention, recognition, or advancement. The applications are as varied as are the people who pray. God knows our weaknesses and places of special vulnerability.

And if we don't pray? Aren't we opening ourselves to situations in life that could overwhelm us? I think so. We recall Paul's words in 1 Corinthians 10:13, assuring his readers that "God . . . will not let you be tempted beyond your strength, but with the temptation will also provide the way of escape, that you may be able to endure it." Yet the decision to walk along this "way of escape" is not automatic. We must still decide to go through that door of escape and walk that way. How many of us have seen the "way" God has shown, known that there we could escape, yet gone in a different direction, to our sorrow? Very few, if any, of those who read these words could deny having had such experiences.

The author of Hebrews urges his readers to draw confidently before the throne of grace, in order to receive mercy and help in time of need (4:16). Those readers, for whatever reason, were tempted to abandon their faith, and the author argued powerfully, encouraging them to avoid this disaster by letting God keep them from falling prey to temptation. Christians sometimes become discouraged by their weaknesses and failures. This passage is a tonic for them, urging them to press on with God's help. He knows our every twinge of weakness and failure but loves us so much that he will keep us from the deadly plunge into sin, if only we will allow him to do so.

Let us note some cases among Jesus' followers that are illustrative of this point. Jesus gave his discourse in Luke 21 about the destruction of Jerusalem and the last things primarily to encourage his followers to be true to him through the struggles and horrors that were to come their way. Attempts to use this passage to construct some series of events by which to foretell the date of the second coming are far off target. The Master's concern was in the spiritual well-being of his disciples. So, among many warnings and encouragements in the chapter, Luke 21:36 says, "But watch at all times, praying that you may have strength to escape all these things that will take place, and to stand before the Son of Man." It is true that Jesus may have spoken of their final appearance before him at the end of the world, but acceptance then could come only if his listeners stood through the threats posed by persecutions, false messiahs, natural calamities, armed conflicts, and the destruction of Jerusalem. Obviously false messiahs and persecutions could be destructive to faith. But so could the other crises just indicated, either by producing a faith-crushing fear or by so filling the mind with earthly concerns that heavenly concerns would be driven out. The destruction of Jerusalem would be devastating to both Jewish and Gentile Christians, because that was the birthplace of the faith. So against all this, Jesus set prayers and the mighty power of God. Modern Christians do well to keep this powerful promise in mind, for our day has its full share of convulsions and distractions that call us away from God. Our knowledge, technological wonders, vast wealth, international power—this word of the Lord speaks of a far greater reality than any of them.

Later, in Luke 22:31–32 (a text only Luke records) Jesus addressed Simon Peter at the last supper: "Simon, Simon, behold, Satan demanded to have you ["all of you" in NRSV—the pronoun here and in the next usage is plural] that he might sift you [plural] like wheat, but I have prayed for you [singular—i.e. Simon] that your faith may not fail; and when you have turned again, strengthen your brethren." The rest of the story shows the impact of Satan's shattering blows on Simon's soul. But though he subsequently denied even knowing Jesus, Simon never left him. The further New Testament story shows Simon's power in the early church. Through the events that buffeted Peter, the stabilizing prayers of Jesus kept him from being completely overwhelmed. Why did Jesus pray this way for Peter and not for the others? The text indicates the greater leadership qualities Jesus saw in Peter. We suppose that Jesus, as the heart-knower, knew that the inner qualities of Simon made him open to this intercession.

This text also returns to a question posed earlier in this chapter. How are we to understand the word translated "evil" in Matthew's version of the Lord's Prayer ("deliver us from evil")? Should we read the term as the "evil one," as Satan? That could be the case in this passage, though the possibility does not prove that it was what Jesus meant. However, reading "evil" as a disembodied force leads us to a view we have rejected, the idea that God would never let sin capture us. The matter is up for debate. Either way, just as Jesus commanded the evil embodied in demonic forces, so in this prayer, Jesus put restraints on what Satan could do.

As we have indicated, there are many ways we need to pray for deliverance from evil. Three of these are indicated by New Testament texts about prayer that regard the temptations of anxiety, temptations connected with marital problems, and temptations posed by persecution. These may be taken as examples of some of the many ways we need to pray "lead us not into temptation."

### ANXIETY

Philippians 4:6–7 says, "In nothing be anxious, but in everything by prayer and supplication with thanksgiving let your requests be known to God. And the peace of God, which passes all understanding, will keep your hearts and your minds in Christ Jesus." God's peace stands at the heart's door, telling worry, "No admittance here!" I happen to have had some memorable personal experience with anxiety. When I was younger, I watched a family member suffer repeatedly with ulcers that were brought on by severe business anxieties, and I determined never to let myself get into a like situation. Some years later, when I became a Christian, I was delighted to find this passage in Philippians that spoke directly to my resolution. Though it would be foolish to say my life has been totally free of worry, I am confident the problem has been diminished enormously by God's answer to prayers.

For many years, I was convinced that worry was a sin, and that was how I preached on the subject. I recall one episode when I knew a harried businessman in the audience was consumed by anxiety over his failing company. I gave him both barrels and let him know he was sinning and needed to substitute prayer with thanksgiving for worry. It was some years later, when I had been blessed with increased insight, that I recognized that I had not relieved his burden but had rather given him one more thing to be anxious about—his "sin" of worrying.

I have come since to reject the position that anxiety is a "sin" and instead to see worry as an affliction rather than a transgression. One could argue that Jesus, praying in Gethsemane, suffered extreme anxiety as he cried out for the removal of the cup of suffering that lay before him. But though he suffered anxiety, he did not sin. Few, if any, humans are free of this affliction. Because individuals have differing emotional makeups, some are more susceptible to worry than others. Some express it openly and volubly; others, just as anxious, keep it deep within. Whether or not God will purge all worry from one's life is not mine to say. I can imagine persons of such great faith that worry has been totally banished from their hearts and minds, but to imagine such persons does not mean they actually exist. In the meantime, we pray with confidence, knowing that the burden of worrisome care will certainly be diminished, and perhaps a specific anxiety will be taken away completely.

There is a saying that worry is like a rocking chair: it takes a lot of time, but never gets you anywhere. Worry can paralyze. It can so fill one's thoughts that no room is allowed for anything else, even for God. It can be about money, or relationships, or danger, or health, or just plain survival. It can be about today's news, or tomorrow's responsibilities. Anyone caught in its grip knows how dominating it can be. Though it is an affliction, it can turn, in myriad ways, into a sin. It drains the joy from life, and makes one center on things that should not be central. Remember Paul's call to be thankful in Philippians 4: 4-7. When we are in a thankful mode, the opposite mode, anxiety, is made to retreat. Peter (1 Pet. 5:7), referring to Psalm 55:22, urged his persecuted brothers and sisters to cast their anxieties on God, "for he cares about you." Christians can stand in this secure place. God may not remove the circumstances creating worry, but he can work in those afflicted and transform them into persons whose hearts and minds are guarded by God's peace.

## Marital Temptations

First Corinthians 7 contains Paul's long discussion of troubled marriages in which one partner was a Christian and the other was not. The chapter is full of puzzling statements, including three that indicate an "impending distress " (v. 26), that the "appointed time has grown very short" (v. 29), and that "the form of this world is passing away" (v. 31). Whatever the nature of this crisis, whether persecution, or the Lord's return, or something else, it gives an urgency to what Paul said regarding various aspects of marriage or potential marriage. The key throughout the chapter is that nothing is to supersede one's relation to the Lord.

Paul's concern in these verses was the sexual aspect of marriage. In verse 5, he said, "Do not refuse one another except perhaps by agreement for a season, that you may devote yourselves to prayer; but then come together again, lest Satan tempt you through lack of self-control." In the preceding verse, Paul indicated that husband and wife had mutual "rights" in their physical relation. In today's culture, we are aware of many of the circumstances that may create problems in sexual relations in marriage. We do not know if Paul had in mind the problems we know, or was thinking of other circumstances unique to the Corinthian context. Yet, he probably recognized that in a sexually saturated culture such as Corinth, physical temptations would be especially strong—as it is even in less worldly contexts. Prayer concern for marriage, whatever the circumstances, is welcome and necessary in any culture.

Peter (1 Pet. 3:7) also counseled prayer in connection with marriage. He called on Christian husbands to live considerately with their wives, honoring them as "joint heirs of the grace of life." Inconsiderate behavior and refusal to honor wives would result in prayer being hindered. Perhaps he meant that problems in the marriage meant that prayer was not given attention or was ignored completely. Whatever Peter's meaning, readers of the present words can certainly see how marital discord can have a negative effect on their own prayers. The most intimate of human relations, where prayer is most needed, paradoxically can become the place where it is most neglected. Many marriages can testify to this, to their sorrow.

Marriage should not be taken for granted, especially for Christians. The invocation of God's aid is imperative. Pray for self control, yes, but also for wisdom, for affirmations of love, for unselfish hearts, for mutual understanding, for communication skills, for a spiritual merging, and for all the other things that are necessary in living together day-to-day. One wonders how many Christians whose marriages have gone on the rocks would have to say, in retrospect, "We just didn't let prayer enter into our relation." Whether man and wife pray together or pray separately, pray they should, and then let God knit them together and keep them from falling into sin when they are apart.

## PERSECUTION

Christians might not pray enough about worry or marital issues, but it is hardly conceivable they would fail to pray when persecuted. Those who live in countries with a substantial "Christian" population probably never see the persecution that runs rampant today, unless it comes in the form of skepticism or ridicule or involves large-scale religious conflict (for instance, the situation in Ireland). But in many parts of the world, especially where Christian evangelism is forbidden, the persecutions visited on believers can be terrible indeed. Much of the New Testament reflects the first-century presence of this animosity, and some books (particularly 1 Peter and Revelation) address it as a major theme. James 5:4 speaks of defrauded Christian farmers and of their cries to God out of their misery. 1 Peter 4:7 calls upon persecuted Christians to "keep sane and sober for your prayers" since "the end of all things is at hand." Revelation 8:3–4 refers to the prayers of the saints, which are mingled with the incense from the heavenly altar.

These three texts, besides assuring persecuted Christians of God's victorious care, let us see their agony (James 5:4) and warn that reactions to persecution could damage their prayer lives (1 Pet. 4:7). None of them gives specific information about how these prayers would be answered. In Acts 4:24–31 and 12:5, 12 (noted elsewhere), we see God's response in blessing the church so the preaching of the gospel would continue.

Though persecuted Christians would wish to be delivered from their sufferings, this was not promised. The early Christians who first prayed "lead us not into temptation" still experienced virulent hostility. But God did imbue them with stamina and courage, as well as the promise of ultimate triumph, so that they would not deny the faith but endure to the end.

## Thoughts to Ponder

1. What is the difference between temptations and trials?

2. Why does God allow us to be tempted?

3. How might God answer your prayer not to be led into temptation?

4. How was Jesus' prayer for Simon Peter answered?

5. Is anxiety a sin or an affliction?

6. Discuss the ways prayer is important in marriage.

# CHAPTER ELEVEN

# THE FRIEND AT MIDNIGHT

The Lord's Prayer is a series of requests. It tells us to come to God as those who ask, and as such, it offers a refutation to those who would belittle prayers of petition. God is a giver who has given us all that we have and who wishes to give us even more. But there is one danger in coming to him with our needs: we must not consider petition the highest use and value of prayer. The highest blessing of prayer is the fellowship with God himself, and the assurance that he is always willing to enter into communication with us. Even if there were no promise of blessings in answer to our prayers, the honor of coming into the Presence and being accepted there at any time would still be the very zenith of human experience. Let us never make our wants and needs more important than God himself, or the relationship with him that he offers us.

## THE AVAILABILITY OF GOD

We find in Luke 11:5–8 a true-to-life story given only in Luke's account

And he said to them, "Which of you who has a friend will go to him at midnight and say to him, 'Friend, lend me three loaves; for a friend of mine has arrived on a journey, and I have nothing to set before him'; and he will answer from within, 'Do not bother me; the door is now shut, and my children are with me in bed; I cannot get up and give you anything'? I tell you, though he will not get up and give him anything because he is his friend, yet because of his importunity he will rise and give him whatever he needs."

Jesus posed a social dilemma to his hearers. Because of a friend's apparently surprising arrival, a host was caught without adequate bread. The host could allow the visitor to go hungry, a serious breach of hospitality, or he could awaken another friend at midnight and ask for help. The second option would also be rude, upsetting an entire household in the middle of the night. Still, the host, unable to bear withholding food from his guest, chose to bother his neighboring friend. The story indicates that the request went beyond the limits of friendship, and friendship did not rise to the occasion, yet the bread was given. Why? The answer is indicated by a Greek word that means, literally, "without shame." The RSV translates it as "importunity"; the NRSV renders it "persistence."

I have seen persistence in prayer powerfully demonstrated in the case of one couple, dear friends and fine Christians, whose marriage had encountered strains that led to an extended separation. Even though it appeared that reconciliation would never occur, one of the partners never stopped praying, even when friends thought the prayers were for the impossible. To the glory of the God who answers prayer, hearts were softened, and now the couple is together again. They have great problems to overcome, but they have committed themselves to the effort, God being their helper.

I can recall times when I attempted to telephone certain very important people, only to be denied access after going through a whole battery of secretaries, receptionists, administrative assistants, and so on. Few of us would pick up the phone and expect to get through to the president of this country for a chat about our needs. More frustrating these days is the attempt to get through the maze of automated messages and seemingly interminable waits to finally speak to a real person—if the last is even possible. How remarkable, then, that at any time we can address the Maker and Ruler of everything and everyone that exists and not experience delay or polite denial. In fact, God even urges us to address him and promises to be always available, even for the least of us. One lesson of the story of the friend at midnight is that we should come boldly to God in prayer. We should not shrink back because of our insignificance, imperfection, or shyness. Unlike the friend, who was doubtless groggy because he was awakened at an inconvenient hour, our Father is always available and caring. We should not hesitate to come into his presence, whoever we are and whatever we have done. He does not sleep or abandon his post.

The interpretation of the word rendered "persistence" in some versions of Luke 11:8 is a valid and important one, and it can be supported by the next few verses, which are Jesus' invitation to ask, seek, and knock. But we also want to look at another way to understand the text. The Greek term when read literally as meaning "without shame" can be understood to refer to the friend in bed, rather than to the person outside knocking. Though it is not the way most translations present the text, reputable scholars (including I. Howard Marshall and John Nolland) have examined the text carefully and expressed a slight preference for this second meaning. Thus, the idea is that the man in bed arises and responds in order to avoid being shamed. Were he not to respond, it would be such a breach of custom and expectation that he would be humiliated in the eyes of his fellow villagers. The onus of his refusal would stain his character in their eyes, and this could reflect on his family as well. No good man would want this disgrace, and thus the inconvenience was endured in order to preserve the giver's honor. This point was probably even more powerful in that culture, with its strong sense of hospitality, than in ours today where a midnight knock on the door could arouse anger or fear.

This interpretation also fits the larger context of the passage. If the man in bed acted as he did for the sake of his honor, how much more are we to know that God will answer our prayers. For God not to respond to prayer would contradict his very nature. He must be a Giver, and he gives all; not to give would be for him to deny himself. It is this gift-nature of God that underlies this text.

This application offers remarkable assurance of God's concern for us and of his desire to bless us. The argument is of the (implied) "how much more" type. If an earthly friend, awakened unceremoniously and rudely, responds out of a sense of honor, how much more will the perfect God, never sleepy, never grumpy, never grudging, the friend always eager to give, answer the prayers of his children!

## THE GREAT INVITATION TO PRAYER

In chapter 5, we focused on Luke 11:9–13 in our discussion of faith. Now our journey has brought us back to these verses. Let us remind ourselves of their content:

> And I tell you, Ask, and it will be given you; seek, and you will find; knock, and it will be opened to you. For every one who asks receives, and he who seeks finds, and to him who knocks it will be opened. What father among you, if his son asks for a fish, will instead of a fish give him a serpent; or if he asks for an egg, will give him a scorpion? If you then, who are evil, know how to give good gifts to your children, how much more will the heavenly Father give the Holy Spirit to those who ask him!

If the story of the friend at midnight taught us in a somewhat concealed form, here the cover is pulled away and Jesus's teaching becomes clear. Whichever person we see as avoiding shame in verses 5–8, in either event we find that "ask," "seek," and "knock" were all features of that story. With some slight differences, the words of verses 9–13 are paralleled in Matthew 7:7–12, but there they are not connected as directly to the petitions of the Lord's Prayer. The setting of these words in Luke seems to offer a smoother context and thus makes the point with greater impact.

Also, the father illustration reappears in these verses. We recall that this was the way the disciples were told to address God in the beginning of the prayer (v. 2). Who could even imagine the shock of a child who, upon asking his or her father for a fish, received a serpent, or who asked for an egg and was given a scorpion? One simply cannot imagine a father practicing such a vile deed on his own offspring. Earthly fathers, though far less than perfect, generally act toward their children with concern and favor. How much more, then, would a heavenly Father, whose very nature is love, bless his children? For any whose primary concept of God deems him to be angry and eager to punish, this text offers a powerful corrective. God is more disposed toward blessing us than we are to blessing ourselves. He knows, far better than we do, which are the real blessings and which the imagined ones. We can always come into his presence with the secure knowledge that he is dedicated to our greatest welfare. To pray is to be embraced by a love beyond any earthly love we can possible know.

I consider this one of the most remarkable and magnificent texts in the Bible. I like to call it the "great invitation to prayer." The normal understanding of the God-man relation sees man as a beggar, pleading for consideration and response, and this is an appropriate perspective. We all come to God like the tax gatherer in Luke 18:9–14, pleading for his mercy to bless our sinful lives. How amazing, then, that in some sense Scripture seems to reverse the roles, showing God as the beggar. Not that we have anything to offer him—instead, he pleads with us to request and accept what he would offer us.

Earlier, we discussed some reasons we do not pray and the importance of praying in faith. Given the invitation to prayer we find in Luke 11, we wonder at the human refusal to accept it. I wonder at *my* refusal to accept it. As I ponder this spiritual puzzle, questions arise:

Do we not have the faith to believe what Jesus here told his disciples?

Are our only prayers those uttered in a "formal" prayer time?

Can a life lived for God be a prayer in itself, even besides "set" devotional experiences?

Can a constant sense of need and gratitude be a sort of prayer?

I hope these are not rationalizations for my own failures in formal, private prayer. They do give hope that I may pray better than I think, but they also shake us into awareness that we have responded only meekly to the invitation Jesus uttered.

Our needs are in every way far more serious than our perception of them; submerged beneath those needs of which we are aware is an ocean depth of real but unrecognized needs. God knows this, and offers to respond to them even before they surface in our consciousness. He will succor us in places where we did not know our weakness. This is a marvel of grace that calls for constant gratitude.

This prayer promise is not limited to Luke 11. Many New Testament texts speak the same message. Jesus' words are found also in Matthew 18:19; 21:22; Mark 11:24; John 14:13; 15:7; and 16:23–24. The promise is expressed by James in 1:5–8, and by John in 1 John 5:14–15. An incredible assurance has invaded our lives. Incredible possibilities open before us. Let us enter. Since the experience of living for God offers such amazing possibilities, it would be a tragedy if we responded only with our heads and not with our entire lives.

## Thoughts to Ponder

1.  Comment on the two ways to interpret "importunity" in Luke 11:8.

2.  As we think about our hidden needs, what needs to surface?

3.  What real but hidden needs have you discovered in your pilgrimage?

# CHAPTER TWELVE

# THE HOLY SPIRIT

"If you, then, who are evil, know how to give good gifts to your children, how much more will your Father who is in heaven give to those who ask him." With only slight differences, this quotation could come from either Matthew 7:11 or Luke 11:13. Most people, if asked to fill in the blank, probably would do so from the more familiar text in Matthew, and read that the Father will give "good things." Thus, it may be a small surprise to see that Luke's account says the Father will give "the Holy Spirit." This difference invites us to consider the relation of the Spirit and prayer as Luke depicted it.

The Gospel of Luke has seventeen references to the Spirit; Acts has fifty to fifty-four, depending on whether certain passages are understood as referring to the human spirit or to God's Spirit. Of these seventy or so texts, many connect the Spirit with prayer. Note the following:

*1–Luke 3:21–22*
Jesus was praying at his baptism when the Holy Spirit descended. The parallel Gospel accounts record the descent of the Spirit, but Luke further indicates this came while Jesus was praying (cf. Matt. 3:16; Mk. 1:9–11; and see John 1:32–34).

*2–Luke 10:21–22*
When the seventy returned from their mission, Jesus rejoiced in the Holy Spirit and prayed.

*3–Acts 4:23–31*
As the threatened church prayed for God to embolden and empower them, the blessing of the Spirit came in answer to their
prayer and led them to continue with the courageous preaching
of the gospel.

*4–Acts 7:55–60*
Stephen, full of the Holy Spirit, prayed for his murderers, in
words reminiscent of Jesus' dying prayer (see Luke 23:34). He
also gave himself into Jesus' hands, which reminds us of Jesus'
prayer, "Into thy hands I commend my spirit" (Luke 23:46).

*5–Acts 13:1–3*
While the church was worshiping and fasting, the Spirit directed
them to set apart Barnabas and Saul for mission work. They were
set apart and sent off on their mission with fasting and prayer.

Other texts in which prayer and the work of the Spirit are connected are
Luke 1:10–15, 64–79; Acts 1:16, 24–25; 6:3–6; 8:14–15, 24; 9:11, 17; 10:3,
4, 9; and 11:5, 12.

Clearly Luke is showing that the work of the Spirit and the prayers of
God's people are intertwined. At the risk of sounding irreverent, I would
suggest that the Spirit is in human life to *do* something. Certainly the very
fact of being indwelt by God himself is a wonder beyond imagining, but God
lives within us to act through us. If someone should claim to have the Spirit
within, my response is to ask them what the Spirit is doing in his or her life.
What is the point of having the Spirit if no consequence is forthcoming?

Generally speaking, Luke is telling us that the Holy Spirit empowered
the early Christians to do the things that God called them to do, and
Luke focuses heavily on evangelism. By comparison, in Paul's writings
the Spirit seems to be more involved in the inner development of the
Christian. (See, for example, Gal. 5:16–24.)

So when Jesus promised the Holy Spirit as the answer to prayer in
Luke 11:13, we believe he was saying that God answers prayer and the
Spirit is the medium through which that answer is given. When Christians pray and God responds, there the Holy Spirit is at work. Luke 11:13
is not an instance instructing non-Christians to pray to receive the Spirit
in some kind of conversion experience, since, as we have noted, this is the

prayer for those who have already chosen to follow Jesus, those who call God "Father." Nor is it a prayer for some second gift or measure of the Spirit. It is, rather, the way God responds to any prayer of any Christian.

Since Luke shows his readers that prayer is answered through God's Spirit, it is appropriate to observe the working of the Spirit throughout Luke and Acts. In that way, we gain insight into ways God can bless and empower his church in all ages. Every major character in Luke and Acts specifically is said to be empowered by the Spirit. John the Baptist was filled with the Spirit from his mother's womb (Luke 1:15). Four times Luke shows the Spirit in Jesus' early career: at his baptism (3:21–22), through the temptation (4:1–2—note the Spirit led him *in* the wilderness, not just *into* it), in his early preaching (4:14, 15), and as the one anointed by God who does the works of the Messiah, as foretold in Isaiah 61:1–2 (4:18–21). Acts 10:38 describes Jesus' ministry as one anointed with the Holy Spirit and power. The twelve received the Spirit on Pentecost (2:1–4). Stephen, the first Christian martyr, was blessed by the Spirit in 6: 3, 5, 10; 7:55; and see 7:51. Philip, another of the seven of Acts 6, was also Spirit filled (6:3, 5). Saul of Tarsus received the Spirit at his baptism (9:17) and was filled with the Spirit when he opposed the false prophet Bar-Jesus (13:9).

Every believer who repented and was baptized in Jesus' name received the gift of the Spirit (Acts 2:38). The remaining verses of Acts 2 (42–47) show the amazing results in the lives of the Spirit-imbued believers. They showed a remarkable generosity, a strong care for one another, a desire to learn and praise God together, a vibrant joy, and a powerful outreach to others. When we consider that many of these were previously strangers to one another, who came from all over the Mediterranean world (Acts 2:7–11), this unity and energy is indeed impressive.

As we move through Acts, the role of the Spirit in energizing the early church is an inescapable element of the text. After he was raised Jesus' instruction to his followers was to wait for God's power. In that power they were to preach repentance and remission of sins to all nations (Luke 24:45–49). In Acts 1, the power is identified as the Spirit (vv. 5, 8), and Jesus' promise was fulfilled with the dramatic events of Acts 2:1–13. Thus began the new age—the age of the Spirit (2:11).

Acts records the triumphs and difficulties of the early church. After the vibrant picture of 2:42–47, noted above, we find some dark times.

### Persecutions

After Peter and John were arrested by the Sanhedrin council and were imprisoned overnight, they were called before the council to explain by what power or name they had "done this" (healed a lame man). Peter, who scant days before had denied even knowing Jesus, now made one of the most courageous speeches recorded in the Bible (4:8–12). The secret to his bold defense was that he was filled with the Holy Spirit (4:8). Before he was through with this striking speech he had, as one writer remarks, excommunicated the entire Sanhedrin, making it clear the only way for them to return to communion with God was by following Jesus. This episode was a striking fulfillment of Jesus' promise in Luke 21:15 ("I will give you a mouth and wisdom . . . .").

When the council demanded that the church stop preaching, it was by the power of the Spirit that they refused to be intimidated and continued to speak God's word with boldness (4:24–31). It was after this that Stephen became embroiled in the debate with certain synagogue members in Jerusalem that finally led to his death by stoning. But his death was really a victory, a victory won through the power of the Spirit (6:3, 5, 10; 7:51, 55). The powerful working of the Spirit in his martyrdom showed that not even execution of the disciples could halt their dedication in preaching.

### Immorality

Those who operate under the illusion that the church was once perfect would do well to consider the case of Ananias and Sapphira. As it has in all subsequent ages, the fledgling church also had its worldly members who did not live the life Jesus had taught. In this case, a man and wife, moved both by greed and by a desire for praise, misrepresented their gift made to the church for the care of the needy. To their shock, they were informed by Peter that their sin went beyond deceiving humans and was an offense against the Holy Spirit (5:3, 9). The church, as an entity indwelt by God's Spirit, thus differs from any other group of humans. The seriousness of the Christian ethic and its violation are indicated by the successive deaths of both Ananias and Sapphira. We must take the sanctity of God's Spirit in absolute earnest. The Spirit not only gives courage under persecution, it speaks to the purity of the church.

## DISSENSION AND DIVISION

Contemporary believers who are distressed over divisions in the body of Christ would do well to pay special attention to 6:1–7. This flap occurred in Jerusalem because some widows were somehow neglected in the daily distribution of food for these needy women. Certainly this was a most serious matter, especially for the hungry sisters, but it also may have been the presenting cause for older rivalries between groups of Jews—now Christian Jews. The apostles, recognizing the imperative need for prayer and the power of the Spirit in resolving this difficulty, set apart seven men who were notable for the way the Spirit worked in their lives. These men worked to resolve the matter while the apostles continued devotedly in prayer and the ministry of the word (v. 4).

Whatever the exact procedures followed, the Spirit worked through the seven and the problem was resolved. The first church division was healed, and evangelism continued. In fact, it continued so remarkably that, for the first time, a "great many" of the priests in Jerusalem accepted the new faith (v. 7). Even the clergy were being converted. The church, with its sorry record of division over the centuries, would do well to consider its history of devotion to prayer in such times of rupture. It is clear that division is not only an affront to Jesus, it also defies the unitive energy of God's Spirit. One might suspect that in such divided circumstances the church has abandoned God's power in order to rely on its own power, marking tragic departures from divine power to destructive human weakness.

Speaking to a similarly divided congregation in 1 Corinthians 3:16–17, Paul reminded his readers, "you are God's temple, and . . . God's Spirit dwells in you. If anyone destroys God's temple, God will destroy him!"

## LEADERSHIP

The Spirit was also active in other areas of early church life. When Paul delivered his farewell speech to the Ephesian elders (Acts 20:18–35), he indicated that the Holy Spirit had made the elders overseers of the church. There are a number of questions about this leadership role that this text leaves unanswered, but we can certainly conclude that the Spirit only confirms overseers when leaders and their relation to the church harmonize with all we can know today of God's will—revealed through the Spirit in the Scriptures. This demands that the church pay critical attention to the Scriptures and devote itself fervently to prayer. Since so many church problems spring from leadership deficiencies, and since so much benefit can be mediated to the church by godly and Spirit-blessed leaders, the church cannot afford to take lightly the appointment of leaders. Even as Paul saw potential problems within the Ephesian eldership (20:28–31), so in every age, carelessness in seeking God's will can be devastating to the church. Many readers will be able to relate their own horror stories of such situations. All kinds of damage can be done to the church, not the least of which is the cessation of evangelism, which is one reason Acts 6:7, about the conversion of the priests and others, is such a powerful statement: God would not allow potential division within the church to stifle this outreach!

### OUTREACH AND EVANGELISM

We discussed this topic earlier in conjunction with the prayer, "thy kingdom come." Its importance is underlined in Acts, since here, the work of the Spirit shows most of all. The Spirit was often active in bringing the Christian message and the prospective convert into conjunction. Acts is largely about conversions to Christ, and in this, the Spirit again and again played a prominent role. Witness the following:

*1–The Ethiopian Eunuch (8:27–40)*
This important official, likely one who accepted the Jewish belief system but who was not a full proselyte, was converted to Christ in a remarkable way. The story demonstrates the appeal of the gospel message to people in high places. It is also shows how the persecution in Jerusalem, rather than halting the gospel, only stimulated its spread. The surprising meeting on a desert road and the subsequent baptism of the eunuch are well-known events, but note that it was the Spirit that urged the preacher, Philip, to approach the eunuch's chariot (v. 29) and to engage in the teaching that followed. Once the baptism was complete and the eunuch joyfully continued his journey, the Spirit "caught up" Philip, and he traveled north along the coast.

Notice, too, that God's guidance is often expressed in other terms, for in verse 26 it was an angel who instructed Philip to

travel south to the place where the encounter took place. I suspect that references to an angel, or to a vision, or to the Spirit,
may all be ways of describing the same basic divine influence.
God knew that a receptive nobleman was on a certain road at a
certain time on a certain day, and he saw to it that a preacher was
there to tell him about Jesus.

### 2–Saul (9:1–31)

When the distraught Saul had agonized with prayer and fasting
for three days, the Christian preacher, Ananias, brought him the
welcome news about God's concern for him. In 9:17, Saul was
told that Jesus had sent Ananias so Saul could regain his sight and
be filled with the Holy Spirit. Here, the Spirit was God's gift to a
convert, just as promised in Acts 2:38. Later, in Acts 9:31, once
Saul's persecution had ended and much of the threat that had so
burdened the church was removed, we are told that the church
in Judea, Galilee, and Samaria was comforted by the Holy Spirit.
Though not directly an evangelistic text, this note describes another aspect of God's power working within the church, which
must have been a special joy that came to those whose lives were
secure in blessings given by a risen Lord—a joy that transcended
the tragedies resulting from the persecution.

### 3–Cornelius (Acts 10:1–11:18)

This extremely important episode, the first conversion of a Gentile
to the Christian faith, is punctuated all through with divine initia-
tives. The first reference to the Spirit appeared when Peter was told
to accompany the Gentile messengers whom Cornelius had sent to
him (vv. 10, 19). Prior to this passage, we read of the prayers both of
Cornelius (vv. 1, 4) and of Peter (v. 9). Further, God sent an angel to
Cornelius and a vision to Peter in order to bring them together.

Peter's preaching about Jesus to Cornelius and those gathered in his house was an historic moment. Christianity was hov-
ering on the brink of admitting non-Jews into the chosen people
for the first time. At that instant, a dramatic divine action made
it clear that non-Jews could be God's people without being cir-
cumcised. God sent the Spirit upon all "who heard the word,"
creating amazement among the Jewish Christians and leading

them to call for the baptisms of those whom God had obviously approved (10:44–48). This once-in-history event, when the Spirit descended on people before baptism, did not "save" the Gentiles, but it made it unmistakably clear that now any person, regardless of background, who feared God and did what was acceptable to him (v. 31) could become part of Christ's body.

Later when Peter returned to Jerusalem, he was called to account for his fraternizing with Gentiles. He defended his actions by telling his critics that he was simply accepting God's leading through the Spirit (11:12, 15–16). This conversion of Gentiles crossed a great gulf for Christianity and made it a universal faith.

### 4–Paul's Missionary Tours (13 and 16)

The greatest evangelistic efforts recorded in Acts are Paul's missionary tours, into Asia Minor and southern Europe. We have already pointed out that God inspired these journeys through the Spirit, in the context of the worship and prayers of the church in Antioch (13:2–4). One of the first hindrances to Paul's preaching came in Paphos, on Cyprus, where Elymas, a false prophet, opposed the gospel message. Paul's decisive judgment upon this man was accomplished because Paul was filled with the Holy Spirit (13:9). Some weeks later, when Paul was forced out of Antioch of Pisidia due to Jewish opposition, we are told the disciples were filled with joy and with the Holy Spirit (13:52). After Paul's expulsion from the district, one might expect the church to be disheartened, but the opposite was true, because it was God, not any man, whose presence made the church joyful, even in the face of difficulty.

One other time, on Paul's second journey, we are told of the Spirit's guidance. This time, though, the Spirit (called in 16:7 "the Spirit of Jesus") forbade Paul to go either due west or northeast from central Asia Minor. This divine pressure drove him to Troas, in northwest Asia Minor where he received the "Macedonian vision" (16: 9–10) that led him across into Europe and to the beginning of important evangelism there. In this case, we see God compelling Paul into new areas and to a wider dissemination of the good news about Jesus.

*5–Baptisms by Apollos (18:24–19:7)*

The essential role of the Holy Spirit in the life of the church is shown in the case of twelve men apparently baptized by Apollos, who was a dynamic follower of Jesus but had never learned about baptism in the name of Jesus for the gift of the Holy Spirit. In short, his knowledge included John's baptism but did not stretch as far as Christian baptism. It is not beyond reason to imagine such semi-Christian groups existing throughout the Mediterranean world, even in Luke's day. The twelve men in 19:2, though baptized for the forgiveness of sins (as John did—Luke 3:3), had not received the Spirit. And though it may seem unnecessarily repetitious, they needed to be reimmersed to receive the Spirit. Whether or not this repetition commends itself to our human reasoning, God in his wisdom did not bestow the Spirit until people were baptized in Jesus' name. There are several lessons in this story, but the one of significance for us in this discussion is that Christians must have the Spirit to empower them to be what God calls them to be and do. Failure is sure for the Christian who lives only by human power, since Satan is more powerful than any Christian. But the indwelling Spirit is infinitely more powerful than the Tempter, and thus makes possible not only the victorious living of the Christian life, but also the powerful doing of God's work among men.

We have demonstrated that Luke and Acts makes the connection between prayer and the Holy Spirit most explicit. Not all of the passages we have just discussed specifically mention prayer and the Spirit in the same context, but when Luke so consciously joins the two in his story of the early church, the link provokes us to think of the one whenever the other is mentioned.

Though Luke and Acts say so much about the subject, there is much in the rest of the New Testament that bears witness to the importance of the Spirit in Christian experience. In the writings of Paul alone, there are over ninety references to the Spirit. Seventeen of these are centered in Romans 8, especially in the first half of the chapter. Others can be found in 1 Corinthians 2, 1 Corinthians 12, 2 Corinthians 2, and Galatians 5:16–25. All of these texts can be read with profit if we keep the importance of prayer and the Spirit in mind, but to explore them all is beyond the limits of our present study. However, we do want to focus for a moment on Romans 8:26–27. Paul wrote:

> Likewise the Spirit helps us in our weakness; for we do not know how to pray as we ought, but the Spirit himself intercedes for us with sighs too deep for words. And he who searches the hearts of men knows what is the mind of the Spirit, because the Spirit intercedes for the saints according to the will of God.

Throughout Romans, Paul had been discussing human weakness. He wrote of the weakness of continual assaults by the flesh on the Christian and the weakness of suffering (8:18–27). This moved Paul to speak of hope (vv. 24–25) and after this to the intercession of the Spirit (vv. 26–27).

Now let me make a personal confession. In the years through which this book has been in process, and through thousands of hours of reflection about prayer, I have often wondered if I understood the matter at all. What is this gift of prayer? Why is it given? Have I understood it effectively? Do I trivialize it? Do I fully recognize the mystery involved? Are my concepts truly God-centered? I only venture to write because the task must be done, and I hope that what I say can be tested against the views of others, and thus we humans can draw nearer to the truth.

I believe most of us recognize our limitations, so when we read Paul's words about weakness, we can connect personally with what he said. We are weak! Even though we may not even fully understand our weakness, we affirm its reality. And we have a communication problem with God. There are various reasons this is so. We certainly cannot fully understand the one to whom we pray. Indeed, we understand only a tiny bit about him—that which he has revealed, and not all of that. Nor do we fully understand ourselves. So we are (partially, at least) uttering prayers out of mystery into mystery.

Our weakness also indicates the helplessness we must feel before God. For what should we ask? Of course, we have the guidance of the Lord's Prayer, as discussed in previous chapters. But even those petitions have nuances that sometimes baffle us. For example, as we pray for him to make us more loving, just what is the most loving perspective in any given life situation? Just what is God "up to," and how might we best fit into those plans? We may think we have a clear vision, but we may be mistaken. So how do we pray?

Though all this discussion may seem to discourage any prayer at all, this is not my intention. Our frailty simply underlines the reality of our lives and calls us to greater humility and to a fuller understanding of God's grace. God knows our weaknesses, but invites us to call on him regardless. No doubt the more we grow in Christ the better we will pray. But our best is still a mutter against the full volume of divine purpose. Rather than a divine word saying, "how dare you pray, you ignorant weaklings," we find a mighty reassurance that God himself, through the Spirit, steps into the picture to strengthen and heal our weak and sickly prayers.

Another view often taken of this text is worth considering. This view acknowledges that deep needs and desires are buried in our souls that we cannot bring to the fore at prayer times. In fact, some of these may not even be matters we clearly recognize, for we are often strangers even to ourselves. But God's Spirit, with supernatural perception, plumbs those recesses of our beings where not even we may have vision ourselves. The Spirit makes our prayers deeper and more complete than we realize. Though we may not articulate a particular request at the prayer time, more is being carried to God than we know or dream. To beleaguered Christians who feel guilty because they do not pray as well as they think they should, take heart: God's Spirit is taking care of the matter.

Here is a marvel. When we combine this Romans text with Luke 11:13, we find God's Spirit active in our prayer lives coming and going. He gives us supernatural aid as we pray, and, as prayer is answered, the response comes through the Spirit's agency. Thus, the prayer act, often seen as a human enterprise, is, in fact, a joint effort of the human and divine from beginning to end.

The work of the Spirit will always be mysterious, and the New Testament connects it with what many moderns consider bizarre manifestations (see 1 Cor. 14). Because of certain contemporary perspectives on the New Testament, extreme views often obscure a biblical picture of God's working through his Spirit. One extreme is to engage in tunnel vision with regard to the gifts of the Spirit (which include tongues, healings, and prophecy) and to focus on them far more than the New Testament does, even to the exclusion of other important aspects of the Spirit's work.

This is an imbalance I have tried to correct by the survey of texts in Acts earlier in this chapter. It is important to remember that most of what we read about the gifts in 1 Corinthians 12 and 14 was written because of problems and abuses in the practice of those gifts.

As a slight aside, one sometimes hears prayers addressed to the Holy Spirit. Certain hymns and Christian songs also exhibit this character- istic. This is defended, I suppose, by realizing that God is three in one, and whether prayer is addressed to Father, Son, or Holy Spirit does not matter. Perhaps so. We do not wish to pick religious nits. But it is true that in the New Testament, prayers are generally addressed to the Father; in a very few cases, they are addressed to the Son (Acts 7:59, and perhaps 1:24). But in no case is the Spirit the addressee in prayers. As we have seen, the Spirit is the empowering function of God, in the praying and God's answering. It seems likely that prayer to the Spirit misunderstands the Spirit's function in the prayer process. Of course, God decides whom he does and does not hear, but we would do well to respect the silence of the New Testament as we address God. Praying to the Spirit does *not* make us more spiritual. It is certainly not a necessary way to pray, and I wonder why it should be done at all.

Still, another extreme approach to the Spirit reacts against the first, the preoccupation with Spirit. So afraid of the excesses of the gifts-focus, this approach hardly mentions the Spirit at all. My own religious commu- nion tends to be at this extreme, and until recent years, our congregants heard little about the work of the Spirit.

We ought to understand clearly that the Spirit is God's gift. It is not subject to human demand or manipulation. When the Spirit acts in response to prayer, it is only because of God's gracious care and not as a result of human obedience. All concern with the Spirit must hold God and his glory, not man and his enrichment, paramount. Some re- actions to God's working almost seem to forget the greatness of God in emphasizing the human indications of what has been received. Some even go so far as to ascribe second-class status to those whose experi- ence of the Spirit does not manifest itself in certain ways. Though the Spirit is not bound in the way it works, either by human conception or description, I would maintain that often the Spirit's presence is "behind the scenes." Thus, the result of the divine intervention can be seen, but the process leading to that result is hidden from human eyes. In some cases the process may even seem to be a "natural" one, though the eye of faith knows otherwise.

We all need to recognize that the Spirit will and does work, regardless of the terminology used to describe God's action. When Christians pray and prayers are answered, there the Holy Spirit is at work, no matter how the process is described. Some may refer simply to God's power, but the spiritual reality remains the same. I maintain that in some Christian experience, the Spirit is at work even where it is not recognized as being effective. I suspect God extends his grace even to those whose vocabularies may be more limited than that of the New Testament.

## Thoughts to Ponder

1. Does Luke 11:13 justify a non-Christian in praying for the Holy Spirit? Why?

2. React to the idea that the Spirit is in human life to do something.

3. React to the idea that the Spirit is the agency through whom God answers prayers.

5. Would you agree that Acts 2:42–47 pictures what happens when the Spirit is at work in the church?

6. According to Acts, how does the Spirit work in conversion?

7. How do you understand Romans 8:26?

8. What about praying to the Holy Spirit?

# CHAPTER THIRTEEN

# THANKSGIVING

Sometimes, when I have argued that the Lord's Prayer is a covering prayer under which all other prayers are considered, I have been asked why I have not included prayers of thanksgiving. Recall 1 Timothy 2:1, where "thanksgivings" are specified as one type of prayer. One answer I have given is that the Lord's Prayer is about requests, which are different kinds of prayers than thanksgivings. Another response is to suggest that an element of thanks is *implied* by calling God "Father." However, the matter does call for further attention. When we examine New Testament prayer texts, the frequency of thanksgivings is quite impressive. When we analyze the Christian life, we discover that a thankless Christianity is, to a large extent, false. Further, it is my conviction that the greatest possible motivation to living Christianly is gratitude. What sort of feeble thing do we have if our faith does not spring from the deepest motivation?

Haven't thanks been intrinsic to the Judeo-Christian history from the very beginning? One might argue that lack of gratitude for the bliss of Eden was one spur behind the eating of the forbidden fruit. And are not all those altars the patriarchs erected testimonies to thankful hearts making offerings to the God who had blessed them? Run through the entire story of redemption, and evidences of gratitude or ingratitude mark the course.

We could write volumes drawing just from thanksgiving texts in the Old Testament. Foregoing that, let us look at the Psalms. If one were to work through all one hundred and fifty, it would be most instructive to see how many involve thanks in some way. About one third of the Psalms are hymns, which center in the praise of God. He is praised for his role in the history of his people, for the kingdom, for Zion, for his care for his people, or for specific blessings (such as good crops, families, and victories). In addition to these hymns of praise, another ten to twelve psalms are specifically designated psalms of thanksgiving, both for individual and for community blessings. Praise and thanks are bound together. Praise is preceded by thanks. Any attempt to praise a God to whom one is not thankful would be superficial and hollow—perhaps even hypocritical.

Let us settle on Psalm 50, in which thanks is given a central place. This psalm begins with a stirring depiction of God issuing a summons to heaven and earth, calling them to witness his fiery coming in judgment on his people (vv. 1–6). God's first charge against Israel dealt with animal sacrifice. He would refuse their animal offerings, for "every beast of the forest is mine, the cattle on a thousand hills" (v. 10). The psalm continues the divine speech with the words, "if I were hungry, I would not tell you; for the world and all that is in it is mine" (v. 12). God charged the people to offer a sacrifice of thanksgiving, or, as an alternate translation, to offer thanksgiving as a sacrifice (v. 11). Then, in time of trouble, they were to call on the God who would deliver them.

What was the problem? Apparently, the people did not understand thanksgiving. Rather than being appreciative for what God had given them, they felt they had something of their own to give to God. They assumed God would be in obligation to them for their offerings—a huge error, completely perverting the true nature of the God-man relation. Thanks only goes one way in this relation, from man to God. There is nothing man can give God for which God offers thanks to man. Even man's decision to serve God is possible only because God gives man the ability to make that choice.

Did what the Israelites were doing matter? It mattered tremendously, since to turn the relation to God upside down destroyed the very nature of that relation. It put man at the center. But that is an illusion, an impossibility. It leaves a pseudoreligion drained of the central gratitude that motivates response to God. Psalm 50 is one of the most powerful affirmations of this truth. God is the giver, man the receiver. The nature of things can be no other way. One of man's basic words to God must always be "thank you."

Thus, as we talk about prayers of thanks, we are led to the deeper level of attitude. A prayer of thanks comes most sincerely from a heart deeply impressed by its recognition of complete dependence on God. We see his hand in nature. We see it in our relationships. We see it in his material provisions. We see it in spiritual blessings. We see it even in adversity. Such a vision means that we submit our egos more fully to his direction. We are less selfish. We become greater servants. We develop the mental perspective that says of all of life, "this is from the hand of God." If my own experience is any measure, it is a slow process by which we enlarge our sense of gratitude. But it is a rewarding journey, and as we learn the truth of gratitude, a continually increasing glory invades our lives.

If we wait to pray until we are perfected in our sense of thankfulness, we might never come to the prayer hour. We do the best we can when we can. But the entire Christian experience is a gradual progress. One of the joys of living life in Christ is the process of growth over the years.

Since prayers of gratitude are so basic, let us speak more broadly about a sense of thankfulness. Then we can apply our observations to prayer. Two New Testament texts come to mind. In the first, Jesus said, "But love your enemies, and do good, and lend, expecting nothing in return; and your reward will be great, and you will be sons of the Most High; for he is kind to the ungrateful and the selfish" (Luke 6:35). It appears that the reception of certain blessings from God is not predicated on whether humans appreciate them. God's gifts can be received in an unthinking, unappreciative, man-centered way. Humans may even feel they enjoy them by right. If so, such individuals have bought into one of the greatest lies by which humans can be victimized. Even when they are deceived, they still enjoy God's kindness. But how much more will those who are grateful be blessed!

The second text, Luke 17:11–19, tells the story of Jesus delivering ten lepers from their affliction. Nine, when cleansed, went their way, with no apparent thought of gratitude to the Lord. But one ex-leper returned to thank Jesus for his deliverance. To the horror of any ethnocentric Jews, this man was a Samaritan, while the other nine were Jews. Not only was the Samaritan the one who responded to the great blessing, but it has been suggested that in that culture thanksgiving indicated his desire for a further relationship to Jesus. The Jews left, apparently unconcerned about Jesus once they had been cleansed. But the Samaritan sought more. Which of the two parties truly desired to follow the Master?

Jesus marveled at the absence of the nine, and commended the foreigner with the words, "rise and go your way; your faith has made you well" (v. 19). Some commentaries suggest that "made you well" indicates he received forgiveness and salvation, as well as healing. Whether or not this was the case, the story shows that faith and blessing are completed by thanksgiving. Without thanksgiving, the circle of man's relation to God is incomplete.

When considering personal dimensions of these passages, I realize the issue is not just my prayers, but me. It is hard for me to be grateful if I assume I am entitled to what God gives. My own grasp of this sin comes when I think of my teen years and how I expected my parents to care for me, without appreciating their gifts. Only in later years did I feel shame for having been such an ingrate. We must *not* make the mistake that says God owes us.

Many of us also have a faulty idea of our own sufficiency, which minimizes our sense of need. But whether we feel our needs or not, they are always desperately present. Life itself, the factors that sustain it, the things that bless it, even the trauma that batters it—all are present only because God so designs. If I feel no need and if I think I am completely self-sufficient, I have no cause to be grateful. But being a Christian means that we recognize our needs at a deep level. Our needs of a spiritual nature are even more urgent than others, though many people have managed to narcotize themselves into denying this. In short, to express prayers of thanks, we must experience an inner transformation, a completely different outlook on life.

Besides the gratitude texts connected with prayer, there are a number of non-prayer passages expressing thanks. In fact, one could nearly say that the entire New Testament is immersed in the waters of thankfulness. Consider the following texts:

*1–1 Corinthians 14:16–17*
"Otherwise, if you bless [give thanks to God] with the spirit how can anyone . . . say . . . 'Amen' to your thanksgiving. . . .

For you may give thanks well enough, but the other man is not edified."

*2.–Ephesians 5:19–20*
"Addressing one another . . . singing . . . always for everything giving thanks in the name of our Lord Jesus Christ to God the Father."

*3–1 Thessalonians 5:18*
". . . give thanks in all circumstances."

These texts make it clear how tightly thanks was woven into the fabric of the Christian faith, not only as an important exercise but as a continuous practice. It was an "all of life" kind of thing.

Now we will consider New Testament texts that indicate thanks for specific blessings in order to understand the lives of the early Christians and to scrutinize our own prayer lives. Since mealtime prayers are one of the most common forms of prayer, let us consider them as a place to enter this discussion.

## PRAYERS AT MEALTIMES

This practice, characteristic of the Jewish faith, was continued by Christians, both Jewish and Gentile. Consider Romans 14:6: "He who eats, eats in honor of the Lord, since he gives thanks to God." False teachers taught, wrongfully, abstinence from "foods which God created to be received with thanksgiving by those who believe and know the truth" (1 Tim. 4:3, and cf. vv. 4–5. But 1 Corinthians 10:30 says, "If I partake with thankfulness, why am I denounced because of that for which I give thanks?"

As with most religious practices, this mealtime thanksgiving can become a ritual and lose its significance. I sometimes wonder if this is so with the public prayer of thanks when dining out. I often have suffered an embarrassing pause when eating with others, wondering "do they, or don't they?" Then, I wonder if it is a genuine act, or a meaningless ritual? Or is it even a showy form of faith? Do some folks feel God will condemn them if they don't? These are somewhat skeptical observations, but they will be worthwhile if they lead us to a more significant time of prayer. Certainly many such prayers are devout. But if they have lost their meaning, it is well that we recognize and correct the situation.

Of course, prayers at home meals are also subject to the fate of unthinking repetition. There are homes where the same prayer, with exactly the same words, has been repeated hundreds, even thousands, of times. This is fine if the words are genuine expressions. But it is problematic if they involve turning on the mouth while turning off the mind.

Meals have great significance. Since the need for food is ever recurring, they afford a continuous call to recognize God's bounty. They signify that God has given us "daily bread." Our meals are not something we obtained by ourselves; they are gifts of grace. To Christians, then, all meals are eaten to the Lord. This brief time of the meal prayer can remind us of all the ways, in every minute of life, we should thank God for what he has bestowed upon us. Even ritual prayer, with its shortcomings, is a better thing than completely ignoring God.

We can see the importance of meals as we examine the Gospels. One might say with regard to Luke that the smell of food is on every page. Often the Lord is found dining with other people, some of whom were curious, some critical, and some devoted. At times, he provided food miraculously. Note that in some communions, the Lord's Supper is called the Eucharist, which means gratitude. *Thanks* began the narratives of the Supper in the Gospels and in 1 Corinthians 11:23–25., and Christians learn that they give thanks for far more than just the elements of the Passover Supper. Likewise, Christian prayers at mealtimes have implications far beyond the provision of food on the table. It is not just bread that we eat; we are tasting the bread of life. Each time we partake, we are reminded of the greater wonder of our forgiven relation to God, made possible by the one who asks us to eat and drink in remembrance of him. We are not suggesting that a "common meal" is the Lord's Supper. But it is a reminder, a lesser hint of the more important meal taken to remember him.

It is worth noting that several mealtime prayers in the New Testament are associated with deliverance. Both the feedings of the five thousand and of the four thousand delivered the multitudes from hunger in circumstances where the normal provision of food seemed impossible (Mark 6:41; 8:6; and cf. parallels in Matt., Luke and John 6:11, 23). In both cases, the Gospels state explicitly that Jesus prayed before the food supplies were multiplied. A scene of even greater danger is presented in

Acts 27:35. Paul, on board ship, spoke to the ship's crew, who had been suffering through a violent storm for two weeks. He urged them to eat and reassured them that God would deliver them from their peril (Acts 27:23). Then he prayed before them all and distributed bread among them. The language of the text is highly reminiscent of the words of the institution of the Lord's Supper. In effect, Paul's prayer was testimony about the God who saves. Throughout these prayers, we see the same motif of deliverance that shone forth with greater glory at the Lord's Supper. Thus we are called to realize that when we pray and eat any meal it is from a position of having been delivered. We are thankful not just for *this* food, but also for *that* deliverance.

## A LARGER LOOK AT THANKSGIVING

Even though they are integral to many of our lives, mealtime prayers constitute only a small part of New Testament prayers of thanksgiving. The following listing will show the hearts of the early Christians and can offer insight and guidance to contemporary Christians. Of course, gratitude ranges through all of human experience, and we may find a need to express thanks in many ways not witnessed in the New Testament. But these Scriptures can stimulate our responses.

1. Just as the Old Testament often thanked and praised God for the creation, so the early Christians addressed him as "Sovereign Lord, who didst make the heaven and the earth and the sea and everything in them . . ." in Acts 4:24. Gratitude, though not explicitly mentioned, is certainly implied here, as those in prayer consider not just creation as a physical wonder, but creation as demonstrating divine power.

2. One of the few instances in which we are given the very words of Jesus' prayers is in Matthew 11:25–27 (paralleled in Luke 10:21–22). He thanked the Father that the truths of the kingdom had been hidden from the wise and understanding and had been revealed to babes. The wise and understanding were probably the religious professionals and those who were proudly confident in their knowledge. The babes were the poor, the nobodies, the needy, and others who were open to Jesus' message. I suppose

the real barrier to comprehension was not in the message, or even in some divine filter letting the word through only to certain people. Rather, it was in the receptivity or nonreceptivity of the hearers. Those with the humility and trust to see Jesus as the revealer of the Father were the blessed ones.

The text offers thanks to God for choosing to reveal himself, especially through Christ, rather than being remote and unconcerned about his creatures. A corollary of this gratitude is prayer for God to make *us* babes, open to receive what he has to give us. We give thanks, as well, for the power of this message to transform lives.

3. In the same vein are Paul's words in 1 Thessalonians 2:13: "We . . . thank God constantly . . . that when you received the Word of God . . . you accepted it . . . as what it really is . . . at work in you believers." Later, we will survey texts in which the apostle expressed thanks for specific godly qualities of his brothers and sisters. The discouragements we sometimes experience in evangelism can be offset by thanks for those who are open—and there are always such people who are ready to accept the feast God offers. Jesus himself recognized that many would not accept his word, but that many others would.

4. "Thanks be to God for his inexpressible gift!" exclaimed Paul (2 Cor. 9:15). Sometimes the wonder of God's love overcame the apostle and his emotions burst forth, as here. It was grace that had moved him so—grace shown in the great generosity to which the Corinthians were urged. What a joy to come to that point in life where one can join Paul in this enthusiastic burst of praise. But this was more than just a prayer—it was a powerful surge of celebration leading to overflowing generosity. God's love for us is so great that it unleashes a corresponding love within us, a love that freely bestows on those in need whatever resources we possess and they require.

Paul expressed this same exuberant joy at the conclusion of the great resurrection chapter (1 Cor. 15). Death is terrible, but victory removes its sting. So, "thanks be to God, who gives us the victory through our Lord Jesus Christ" (v. 57). A similar "shout of grateful joy" is found in Romans 7:25.

5. In 2 Thessalonians 2:13, Paul gave thanks to God because he chose his people "from the beginning to be saved, through sanctification by the Spirit and belief in the truth." The gospel extolled here led to lives characterized by "the glory of our Lord Jesus Christ" (v. 14). Do not be moved from it, exhorted Paul. Salvation ought never be taken for granted, and it will not be by those aware of the wonder of their own redemption and transformation by God.

6. John 11:41–42 and 2 Corinthians 1:11. When Jesus stood at the tomb of Lazarus and asked for the stone to be moved, he thanked God that his prayers had been heard. The voice that raised the dead sounded loudly, and the corpse, grave clothes bound, with life restored, emerged from the darkness.

As Paul wrote to the Corinthians (2 Cor. 1:11), he spoke of an affliction so severe he feared it might end his life. In his extremity, he learned an even fuller reliance on the God who raises the dead. But Paul seems to have anticipated further perils in his path, as he urged the Corinthians to help him by prayer. He did this confident of God's answer and foreseeing that such a divine response would lead to thanksgiving by many.

It is both easy and difficult to pray in times of life's grave and endangering circumstances. It is hard because one may feel abandoned by God, and prayer thus seems to be a futile effort. But it is easy because people, bereft of all personal strength and resources, cry out in desperation to the All-Powerful One. Paul's testimony connects thanks with such prayers, because of deliverance, even when the deliverance may not remove the external problem. In such cases, one thanks God for the internal growth that comes only through absolute trust in him during the most trying hours.

As Jesus' prayer was a witness to God's work in him, and as the help given Paul through prayer would lead many to give thanks on his behalf, so our thanks to God for his answered prayers have testimonial effect. When so many collapse and fail before life's traumas, the triumphant Christian response to such circumstances speaks a powerful gospel message to the world.

7. A number of New Testament prayers thank God for the gifts he bestows upon his children. In 1 Corinthians 1:4–5, Paul tells his readers that he thanks God for having enriched them in "all speech and all knowledge." These words lead to a couple of interesting observations. First, Paul departed from his usual compliments of the virtues of his recipients. 1 Corinthians reveals far more about their faults. Yet God had shown them grace, despite their problems. Second, these gifts, rather than being employed to God's glory and the building up of the brothers and sisters, had become divisive because they had been abused (chapters 12–14). But God did not withhold his gifts because of the perversity of the people. In fact, their shortcomings show how much more they needed God's help to make of them what he created them to be.

There may be a lesson here for us when we observe the failures of Christians today. Perhaps we should be thankful that God has not given up on them, or on us. He may even use us as instruments of his generosity. This is not to wink at failures in the faith, but we may be encouraged to be used by God to help rather than just to condemn. Our prayers can thank God for the ways he acts on flawed Christian lives and ask to be part of his bestowal of blessing. We also need to remember that we might be faced with inadequacies so overwhelming that we can find no reason to thank God for what we are, but only for what God has done for us.

Other prayers of Paul do thank God for the virtues of Christians. Whereas the Corinthians had not yet allowed God's gifts to deepen their Christian experience, in many other cases, God's work had significantly affected his people for good. Though there is a natural tendency to be thankful for what one has received personally, the concern for others that is intrinsic to Christianity leads one to be grateful as well for the way God has changed others' lives. The richness of the community experiences of Christians is due largely to the kinds of persons drawn into that fellowship. Paul was profoundly aware of this as he wrote his various letters. Here are the various qualities of fellow Christians for which Paul gave thanks:

### a. Faith

In Romans 1:8; Colossians 1:3; 2 Thessalonians 1:3; and Philemon 5, Paul wrote that he had thanked God for the faith of each letter's recipients. In Romans, Paul specifically gave thanks because that community's faith was proclaimed in all the world. The reputation of the church in Rome had Empire-wide influence. Likewise with regard to churches in Ephesus, Colossae, and Thessalonica—their faith in the Lord was known beyond the local boundaries. These were good people in good churches. In like manner, the apostle noted that he knew the faith of Philemon. In a letter to Timothy, Paul reiterated that the Christian charge is love coming from sincere faith (2 Tim. 1:3–5).

### b. Love

In Ephesians 1:15; 2 Thessalonians 1:3; and Philemon 5, we see that the love of the saints was also a topic of Paul's thanksgiving. Ephesians and Philemon speak of love "for all the saints," and Thessalonians speaks of the "love of every one of you for one another."

### c. Hope

Colossians 1:3, 5 says, "We thank God . . . because of the hope laid up for you in heaven." These words primarily express thanks for what God had done, but secondarily, they speak for those whose lives were affected by God's work. Their hope transformed their lives. So with believers in every age: hope works backward, flowing from the future to transform the circumstances of the everyday.

### d. Concern for Others

In 2 Corinthians 8:16, Paul offered thanks because God put into the heart of Titus the same "earnest care" for the Corinthians that he felt himself.

### e. Generosity

In 2 Corinthians, where Paul discussed the contribution he was gathering for the Judean Churches, he thanked God for the potential generosity of the Corinthians (2 Cor. 9:11–12). Their openness would produce a double blessing: both help for the needy and overflowing thanksgiving to God.

Humans are inclined to be self-centered. Life in Christ reverses this by calling them to be, first, God-centered, and then, other-centered. These prayers reflect the actualizing of that process. Humans also tend to be jealous of others who might surpass them or garner more praise than they do. These prayers also show how God's work can help vanquish this tendency. If Christian prayers are of the sort we have noted here, then the nature of God, the great Giver, will invade and bless his communities on earth. The more we pray in these ways, the more we escape the trap of ego-centricity. There is a marvelous freedom in being able to thank God as freely for the way he has blessed others as we thank him for the ways he has blessed us.

8–Two texts show the deep gratitude Paul felt for the ways in which other Christians shared concern for him. Philippians was written from prison, and in chapter 1, Paul spoke not only of the burden of imprisonment, but also of those trying to make his situation more difficult. He spoke of the possibility that he would die, but he also trumpeted his gratitude for the Philippians' "partnership in the gospel from the first day until now" (v. 5). In this joyful prayer, he was able to rise above the difficulties of his immediate surroundings.

Joy was also a dominant response when Paul thanked God for the Christians in Thesssalonica and for what their fellowship meant to him (1 Thess. 3:9). He was well aware of the power of having others share in the same divine cause for which he was working. Just as God reminded Elijah that he was not alone, even while he despaired in the desert (1 Kings 19), so we should recognize that we are part of a fellowship created by God, and for that, we should offer continual thanksgiving.

9–When Jesus was raised and his disciples were convinced of his resurrection, he called them to the privilege of sharing his love with others—with the evangelistic commission. Had it not been for this, if Christianity had remained a private sect for only a select few, most of us reading now would not now enjoy the blessings of Christian faith. Perhaps no one was ever a more energetic evangelist than Paul. Thus we are not surprised to find him giving thanks for God's working in his outreach, saying, "But thanks be to God, who in Christ also leads us in triumph, and through us spreads the fragrance of him everywhere" (2 Cor. 2:14). In writing to the Colossians, he asked them to pray that God would open a door for declaring the mystery of Christ, and he coupled this request with the injunction to be watchful and pray with thanksgiving (Col. 4:2–4).

## SOME PRACTICAL SUGGESTIONS

Let us close this chapter with some practical remarks. This New Testament listing should not limit the objects of our gratitude. Each life will have its own list. To give a personal example, as I have grown older, I have an increasing number of flashbacks to stupid, inconsiderate, and sinful behaviors in my life. Sometimes in solitude, I find myself blushing when these painful recollections surface. They pop up at the strangest times, and without warning. Despite my embarrassment, they do increase my wonder that God, for these many years, has forgiven me over and over. If I weighed such things on a scale of what I deserve, my case would be hopeless. But I am allowed to weigh them on the scale of his grace, and knowing this, I am moved to a powerful gratitude. This is one of many ways the imperative to thanks has been sent into my life. But this is my list, and it will not be the same as yours. I am suggesting, then, that you reflect on your own reasons for thanksgiving.

- Try this exercise: Make a list of things that come into your life that you are *not* thankful for. I don't mean only bad experiences, but list things for which you are *just not thankful*, for whatever reason. Then begin to think through this list in terms of the great realities of the Christian faith. I won't tell you what ought to be the result of this introspection; you can learn it for yourself.

- Here is another exercise to enhance your sense of appreciation for what God has given: Like the "Top Ten" lists on popular TV shows, make a list of the ten things for which you are most grateful. You can revise as often as you wish. I promise you, it will be a provocative experience. If you want a further twist on the same exercise, make a list of the top ten sources of gratitude that could be possessed also by non-Christians. Then make a top ten list of those things that have come into your life only because of your relation to God. This also should be an enlightening exercise, and hopefully a faith-building one. A practical way to do this would be to list the blessings of nature that all enjoy: the world, this day, food, friends, home, pleasures. Then, on a second list note the blessings of grace and the new way, as God's child, you can see blessings of nature.

- Another way to enlarge the area of gratitude in your life is to tell people you are thankful for them. The more we live all of life with thankful hearts, the more we can weave gratitude at these simple levels into gratitude at the highest level—gratitude to God.

- A more advanced, and more difficult, practice would be to express gratitude for the unpleasant, even for the tragic, elements of life. Illness, defeat, enemies, disappointment—this is a dismal list. Yet these circumstances give us the chance to learn lessons otherwise unlearnable, and to practice Christian virtues in the very toughest times. From these terribly enriching experiences, we can minister to others in truly significant ways. When we can truly say to a fellow sufferer, "I know how you feel," because of our similar suffering—there is great power in such ministry.

Earlier in this chapter, I said that a sense of gratitude is generally a slowly growing thing. Exceptional circumstances may give a growth spurt, but we should not be discouraged if progress seems snailish. Perhaps it is, but surprises await us along the way as old statements take on new significance, and our lives are continually brightened as we learn more and more of the truth.

If we are ungrateful, we make ourselves poorer. Even if we receive the same blessings as we would if we were grateful, we are poorer, for ingratitude lives by a lie. It makes a false and heretical assumption about life. It deceives us into thinking we are independent. A life based on this falsehood is a life headed for destruction. Further, ingratitude keeps us from receiving much of what God wishes to give. If we do not acknowledge need, we will not ask, and if we do not ask, we will not receive. Simon (Luke 7:44–48) missed forgiveness. The elder brother (Luke 10:25–32) missed joy. The Pharisee (Luke 18:9–14) missed an element of mercy. The wicked tenants (Luke 20:16) lost the vineyard.

It has been stated before but cannot be overemphasized: gratitude is the great motivator. It is deep and long-lasting. Guilt or competition may produce temporary results, but they cannot compare with the fruits of thanksgiving. The goal of all Christians should be to rise to the level of constantly thankful lives.

## Thoughts to Ponder

1.  Distinguish thanks and praise.

2.  Discuss the idea that gratitude is the greatest Christian motivator. What other forms of motivation are commonly employed in Christian circles?

3.  How do you feel about prayers of thanks when dining out at a restaurant?

4.  How can we increase our sense of gratitude?

5.  Why is prayer in hours of tribulations both hard and easy?

# CHAPTER FOURTEEN

# PRAISE AND ADORATION

Praise and thanksgiving, if not the same, are closely related. In both cases, the usual assumption is that blessing has been received, evoking thanks or praise as a response. Praise can surpass this situation, though, by concerning itself with what God *is*, more than with what he has done. If ever there was reason to praise and adore, there is such reason with God, both in view of his works and of his very being.

Praise has been defined as an expression of approval or admiration. People commend the object of praise and offer homage. Definitions of adoration are a bit stronger, including the ideas of regarding with utmost esteem, love, and respect, and the paying of divine honor in worship. Experience and Scripture teach us that adoration can be a very emotional experience, but we are not speaking of loose, ungrounded feelings. The foundation is the reality of God's being and deeds, and our emotions can grow from that. And for the less emotional among us, we should add that praise and adoration can be just as valid if they are basically rational rather than emotional expressions.

It is worthwhile to reflect on these matters, lest we confuse verbal outbursts or the constant repetition of praise words without praising hearts in Christian song with genuine praise. We must not make the mistake of thinking excitement alone is praise. At the same time, proper praise may get us very excited indeed.

Now to Scripture. We may find more material on praise in the Old Testament than in the New, especially because of the nature of the Psalms. Beyond the Psalter, however, the Old Testament yields a wealth of material than we can only touch in passing. Praise texts are also found in Torah, narrative material, wisdom literature, and in the prophets. When one begins exploring for such material, the quest soon becomes overwhelming. I began a trip through the Psalter and found praise references in Psalms 7, 8, 9, 16, 18, 21, 22, and in 26 other psalms just in the first seventy-five chapters. I am quite sure that Psalms 76–150 would yield even richer treasures. But even if we were to mine them all, the findings would be far too extensive to include here. Readers might enjoy their own trips through this wondrous landscape.

Praise in the Psalter is particularly found in, but is not exclusive to, the hymns. These comprise about fifty psalms and, upon analysis, show God being praised for good crops, good families, good weather (and bad, for that matter—see Ps. 29), victory in battle, the kingdom, Jerusalem, personal and national deliverances, and answered prayers. Even these do not exhaust the list. Since Israel's faith was this-worldly, devoid of expectations of heaven or fear of hell (so far as Old Testament texts are concerned), reasons to praise, though spiritual, were for material benefits and blessings. In the New Testament, we expect to find a greater focus on blessings of the spirit.

We turn, then, to the New Testament. Our general principle has been to select only praise texts that are prayers, but it is sometimes difficult to know which are meant to be prayers and which are not. If we define prayer as words addressed to God, then these texts do not strictly qualify. They are about God, rather than written to him. In passages like these, it is as if God listens (and we intend him to) as we talk about him. While petitions deal with what we wish God to do, these texts are about what he has done already. We can survey these verses in terms of the reasons God is praised. Generally, they are not about God as he exists apart from man, but they praise him because of what he has done in relation to his creatures.

## SALVATION

The largest category, by far, praises God for salvation. This is expressed in various ways:

- For his mercy in bringing salvation, and for his plan that is beyond understanding—Romans 11:33–36.

- For the salvation of the Gentiles—Romans 15:9–11. This text includes a series of Old Testament quotations, and is also a call for the Gentiles to praise God.

- For revealing the mystery that brings the obedience of faith—Romans 16:25–27.

- To the king of ages, immortal, invisible, only God, the God who saves—1 Timothy 1:17, 15.

- For hope—1 Peter 1:3–5.

- To God who saves through Jesus Christ—Jude 24–25.

- Revelation is written in exalted language about the conflict between God and evil, and about the glorious victory of the Lamb. The book is punctuated with marvelous paeans of praise that express this in various ways—1:6; 4:8; 5:9; 19:1, 5–8.

## BLESSINGS IN CHRIST

Other texts bless and praise God for the blessings given within the framework of life in Christ:

- For the promise of power (the Holy Spirit)—Luke 24:53.

- For strength—Romans 16:25–27.

- For comfort in affliction—2 Corinthians 1:3.

- For a deepened understanding and practice of love, and for power to be God's persons—Ephesians 3:20–21.

## SPIRITUAL BLESSINGS

The most extensive catalogue of gifts of God is in Ephesians 1:3–14. In verse 3, God is blessed for granting every spiritual blessing in the heavenly places. Analysis of the verses following this reveals a marvelous description of the blessed life. God's people are chosen to be holy and blameless (v. 4), are destined in love to be his sons (v. 5), are to live to praise the grace he has bestowed on them (v. 6), are redeemed, are forgiven (v. 7), are made privy to the mystery of his will to unite all things in Christ (v. 9, 10), are given hope (v. 12), and have received the Holy Spirit as a guarantee of the inheritance (v. 13, 14). These verses are a remarkable treasure- house. Any of these descriptions is like a fabulous jewel that increases our wonder the more closely it is examined. No wonder Paul opens this text with "blessed"!

Though the passages we have examined are not strictly prayers, there is no reason such sentiments cannot be part of our prayer expressions. However, when praise becomes prayer, it is usually transmuted into thanksgiving. But what are we to make of the fact that the praise texts in the New Testament are not exactly prayer texts? We would be wrong to interpret this evidence to mean we should not bring God's praise before him in prayer. Humans will, and should, praise God when they pray. How can we not do so? He is the source of all blessing and infinitely worthy of our adoration. In Christian worship, many of our songs are actually prayers, and of these prayers, a good number praise God directly. Meditation on these hymns could well aid us in our nonmusical prayers.

Earlier, we spoke of New Testament praise texts as if God were "standing by," hearing us praise him to others. This suggests a significant aspect of the Christian faith. We are not advocating what we consider a rather tiresome, even exhibitionistic, lifestyle that can hardly speak a sentence without some form of "praise the Lord" slipping out; nor are we suggesting a life that never acknowledges praise to God. Between these extremes, there are appropriate occasions when it is natural for a Christian to bless the God whose love has been given so fully to humans. Paul did not praise God and Christ in every sentence he wrote, but when he did, his words were powerful because they fit so perfectly where he placed them and because they fit so perfectly into life.

Even as a Christian, I am put off by the athlete, interviewed after a game, who must get in a religious statement before saying anything else. I appreciate the person's faith but somehow feel the statement might be a compulsive "salvation by works" action. If I were not a Christian, I suspect I would not be drawn to Christ by these "testimonies," but would be repelled. Some may object to my feelings on this point, and I readily admit I am not the final arbiter in these matters.

But just how *do* we encourage and enhance praise in our lives? Since praise often takes place when Christians meet together, let us make our first stop there. As I have suggested earlier, it is important to understand that encouraging emotion in the assembly does not necessarily produce praise. I suspect I am like you, and hope, when meeting with Christian brothers and sisters, to experience awe, celebration, warmth, or even sadness. If the assembly is emotionally satisfying, I am satisfied. But, honestly, I am not sure I have praised in all these gatherings. Nonreligious meetings have also satisfied me emotionally, though they have no tincture of the praise of God. It is, I believe, a serious mistake to seek only to produce an emotional effect in the assembly. When I hear a worship leader begin a song with, "Now let's really praise," I have to ask whether I am being called to praise or enthusiasm.

There is no doubt, however, that Scripture indicates there can be a clear relation between joy and praise. Many psalms witness this—see, for example, Psalms 4:7; 33:1–2; 63:5; 67:3–5; 71:23; and 95:1–2. Nonetheless, we must not suppose that joy is simply a temporary emotional explosion. It is a far deeper thing, rooted in a solid conviction that, due to a relationship with God, all will be well.

This is no polemic against genuine emotion, which can powerfully enhance not only praise, but also the entire Christian life. But it is an argument against manufactured emotions, such as forced smiles, reluctant hand-holding, or insincere hugs. These manipulative emotions can be shallow, are short-lived, and, most seriously, can lead us to be satisfied with something that is less than the deepest level of praise. Emotions can certainly enhance a genuine praise experience, but they are not necessary for one's praise to be valid and powerful.

If the worth of God is measured against the praise we give him, then the most intense and exalted praise falls almost infinitely short of the Reality. What, then, of us who struggle and sputter in our praise? Perhaps even as feeble as our efforts are, we are not quite so bad as we imagine ourselves to be. God is praised in many ways outside the Christian meeting. Meditation, Christian reading, acts of service, our modes of relating to others, even silence, as well as many other things, may be carriers of praise. An awareness of these avenues reminds us that true praise is not composed of spurts in an assembly, but is an all-of-life activity. It is difficult, if not impossible, to praise God in corporate worship if we are not attempting to do so in the hours outside the meeting. If we are to enhance praise activities when we come together, we must develop such a perspective in all that we are and do. Following this, the corporate worship will flow naturally from the rest of our lives.

How are we to develop praise in our personal lives? As paradoxical as it may seem, we should pray to be able to offer prayers of praise. This means that we will pray to be sensitized to see life in terms of what God has done—in nature and through Christ. After all, the general idea of praise is not foreign to us. We direct it to actors, athletes, politicians, performers, nature, aspects of history, people, and events, well-known and not so well-known. If we will stop and review even one day's activity, we will discover how often praise fills our hearts, for our families, fellow Christians, neighbors, the weather, or vacation. Why do we praise all these things? When we answer this question, we can apply the answer toward our relation to God, which involves a continually Godward-growing perspective. It is a part of the process of growing in Christ. We presume that Christian growth—a part of the joy of living in Christ—will also mean growth in adoration of the One who has saved us.

Although the leap to adoration of God may be too large for most of us to make at one bound, we can begin by developing the praise faculty at lower levels. We can learn to increase in appreciation for what we deem outstanding. We can cultivate a philosophy that values the true, the good, and the beautiful. As we grow, we can move toward the adoration of God. Our training at lower levels puts us into condition to function at the highest level.

Psalm 148 may be instructive here. Its first stanza praises God from the heavens (vv. 1–6); its second praises God from the earth (vv. 7–14). It is the psalm we sing in the hymn, "Hallelujah, Praise Jehovah." Of the thirty or so praising entities in the psalm, only ten are what we consider rational beings. How, then, is God praised by stars, beasts, seas, mountains, or weather? They praise him by being what they are—what he created them to be. So with us. We also praise God by being what he has intended us to be. This does not mean what we have become by our own selfishness and willfulness, but what we are becoming by fitting into what he intended when he created us—by living in relation with him. The point is this: We praise God by how we live. Living as God wishes us to, thinking as he would have us think, speaking as he would have us speak—these are ways in which we praise God, even though we may not utter any specific "praise word." Haven't we all seen lives of which we say, "that person truly lives to the praise of God"? And do not such examples stir us to like behavior?

Thus, the praise of God, unspoken but powerful, is found in the home, workplace, athletic field—in any place God's children are being what he has called them to be. This lived praise is also empowered by prayer.

When such believers come together in public adoration, the occasion is powerful. There is no forced emotion or artificial activity. Rather, from hearts filled with gratitude and steeped in the vision of God's grace, the praise of God soars forth—"Blessed be the God and Father of our Lord Jesus Christ!" It is for praise, in all its forms, that we have been made!

Can a life be a prayer? I am uncertain about the answer, but if it can, I suspect it would be a life of praise. Perhaps people could so live that their very existences would speak a hallelujah. Whatever our lives are, God hears them. But different lives convey different messages. The optimistic young lady, always smiling and ready to help; the quiet older man who always seems to be doing good behind the scenes; the married couple whose home is a place of powerful ministry to children and adults—these, and others, tell me of ways God is praised through lives. Are such lives prayers in themselves? They very well may be.

### Thoughts to Ponder

1. Is praise prayer?

2. What must lie behind public praise?

3. Can praise in the meeting be overdone, to the exclusion of other aspects of worship?

4.  I have heard it said that praise is one of the easiest things we do. Do you agree or not?

5.  What is the role of emotions in praise?

# CHAPTER FIFTEEN

# INTERCESSORY PRAYER

Earlier, in discussing prayer for the sick, we observed that both understanding and praying such prayers is fraught with difficulty. Now as we come to consider prayers of intercession, we are met with complications as perplexing, if not more so, than those in the former discussion. Again we will see a familiar concern loom large: man's free will.

If we could bypass the subject of intercessory prayer, we could avoid some rough places in the road. But we would also be deprived of great riches in our relations to God and to others. It is surprising to note the frequency of these intercessory petitions in the New Testament. There are roughly one hundred New Testament texts where some prayer request is addressed to God, and about one-third of these are intercessions—prayers for someone else. These assume that because one prays *here* something happens *there*. Many of these requests echo those we have discussed in previous chapters. But for the sake of those who would pursue the matter further, I offer the following imperfect categorization.

### PRAYERS FOR THE SPIRITUAL WELFARE OF OTHERS

- Luke 22:31–32. Jesus prayed for Simon Peter, that his faith would not fail, and that he would subsequently strengthen his brethren.

- Romans 15:13. Paul prayed God would fill the Romans with joy and peace in believing, so that by the power of the Holy Spirit, they might abound in hope.

- 2 Corinthians 13:7, 9. Paul prayed for the Corinthians, that they would do right (v. 7) and find improvement (v. 9). Anyone familiar with the troubled Corinthian church can appreciate the thrust of these requests.

- Ephesians 1:17–23. Paul prayed that his readers would be enlightened to further grasp the hope to which God had called them, the riches of God's inheritance in the saints, and the greatness of God's power in believers.

- Ephesians 3:16–19. Paul asked God to grant his brethren inner strength through the Spirit, that Christ would dwell within their hearts through faith, and that they would comprehend the call to love more fully so they would be filled with all the fullness of God.

- Philippians 1:9–10. Here the apostle asked God to increase the love of his readers "with all knowledge and discernment" so they would approve that which was excellent, to God's glory.

- Colossians 1:9–11. This prayer asked for increased spiritual knowledge and understanding, which would result in a fruitful life in the Lord's service. In addition, Paul prayed God's power would strengthen the Colossians for joyful endurance, patience, and thankfulness.

- 1 Thessalonians 3:12–13. Again, Paul offered prayer for the Christians' love for one another to increase, so the Thessalonians' hearts could be established as unblamable in holiness. A similar prayer appears in 2 Thessalonians 3:5.

- 1 Thessalonians 5:25. Paul said, "Brethren, pray for us." The praying apostle also needed to be the prayed-for apostle.

- 2 Thessalonians 1:11–12. Here Paul's request was for God to work in the Thessalonians in every good way so that Christ would be glorified by their lives.

- 2 Thessalonians 2:16. Paul prayed God would comfort the hearts of his people and establish them in every good work and word.

These prayers certainly bear powerful witness to the deep concern of Paul for his fellow Christians. When prayers of this sort flowed from Christians wherever they were found, they demonstrated the incredible bonds of love and concern throughout the church. Would that every age could share this passion of fellowship.

### PRAYERS TO SPREAD THE KNOWLEDGE OF CHRIST

- Ephesians 6:18–19. Paul asked his readers to pray for him (as well as for all the saints), that he would be given boldness in proclaiming the gospel. This text reminds us of the prayer for boldness in proclamation of Acts 4:29, 31.
- Colossians 4:2–4. Paul asked these brethren to pray God would give him an open door for the word, as well as clarity in speaking it.
- 2 Thessalonians 3:1. The apostle's request was for prayers on his behalf so that the word of the Lord could speed on the triumph through him.

### PRAYERS FOR THOSE WHO HAD SINNED

Christians, if they are like their Lord, earnestly desire all people to be saved. But salvation can only come to those who choose to accept it in true faith and repentance. If God were to force forgiveness on those who, by impenitent hearts, refused forgiveness, he would be contradicting the freedom he had given humans when he created them. Yet no person, no matter how depraved, is beyond the reach of God's love if they willingly allow that love to capture them. Each person's life story draws its greatest significance from the "yes" or "no" that person says to God. It is against this background that we should consider the following texts.

- Matthew 5:44 and Luke 6:28. Jesus said, "Love your enemies and pray for those who persecute you" (Matt.), and "pray for those who abuse you" (Luke). In Matthew, praying exemplifies the controlling attitude of love. The same is true in Luke, but the parallels to the call to pray are more extensive, including instructions to "do good" and "bless."

  Though Jesus did not give more explicit content for these prayers, it is clear that whatever we pray should reflect the love that wishes even enemies well. May they have God's blessings, and may they have the greatest of all blessings—salvation. But we know they must repent, so perhaps the person praying should ask for God's empowerment to try to bring that repentance about. The very deepest truth of these texts is that Christ's disciple eschews hatred and a desire for revenge, as Jesus himself did. Negative, self-centered emotions are replaced by positive, God-centered love. This by no means ignores the evil done by the enemy. It hopes, rather, that he or she may somehow be cured.

- Luke 23:34; Acts 7:60. Human teachers who propose higher standards frequently fail to live out their own agendas. But there is magnified power when the one teaching those high standards consistently follows them, particularly when the teacher must endure through a grave crisis. Power increases even more when the teaching is one that is difficult to follow even in the best of times. Imagine, then, the power in Jesus' instruction to love one's enemies when, as he suffered crucifixion agonies, he cried, "Father, forgive them . . ." (Luke 23:34). Certainly his torturers were embraced by this call, but beyond that, we believe his words are universal, announcing a forgiveness made possible for the whole human race because Jesus willingly submitted to his ghastly fate.

  We view Jesus's forgiveness on the cross as a prologue to the story in Acts, beginning with the announcement that even those who crucified the Lord and Christ could be forgiven upon their repentance and baptism (Acts 2:36–38). Even those people who impaled and taunted him in the crucifixion hours were not outside the reach of God's love. One wonders how many of those who were party to the obscenity of the crucifixion later recognized their wrong and surrendered to Jesus as Lord? We do recall that a Roman centurion, as Jesus died, confessed him as the son of God (Mark 15:39).

- Acts 6:5-8:2. As time passed, and as more and more people came to believe in Jesus, opposition to the movement intensified. In this setting we come to the case of Stephen. He is remembered as the first Christian martyr—one who refused to renounce his Lord even in the face of a brutal death. If we place one finger at Acts 7 and follow the story closely, then have another finger at Luke 23, we note how Luke skillfully parallels the death of the first martyr with the death of Jesus. He who died for Jesus died like Jesus. This is especially true with regard to his prayers, as we have noted elsewhere. How well Stephen had learned the lesson his master had taught both by word and life (and death)!

- Acts 8:18–24. Simon the sorcerer, who attempted to purchase the power to bestow God's Spirit, received the severest of rebukes from Simon Peter ("You are in the gall of bitterness and the bond of iniquity"—8:23). He was told to repent and pray that God might forgive him (v. 22). Apparently shaken to the core by these events, Simon said to Peter, "Pray for me to the Lord, that none of what you have said may come upon me." One might question Simon's sincerity and only see him as frightened by a horrible fate (perishing—v. 20). But the tenor of the story implies an earnest response. This episode has been called the "plan of salvation for an erring Christian" and signals us to pray for others in cases where they obviously demonstrate repentance and the desire to be forgiven. Perhaps Simon felt some sense of shame that might hinder his own prayers. He certainly felt and respected the high authority of Peter.

- Romans 10:1. Paul spoke of his Jewish brethren and indicated his prayer for them, that they might be saved. His energy in carrying the gospel throughout the Mediterranean world may be the best comment on this text. It might be understood as meaning, "bless me, as I carry the saving message to them."

- 1 John 5:16. One is to pray for those not guilty of mortal sin (literally sin toward death), in hope such people would be given life. Regarding mortal sin, John says, "I do not say one is to pray for that." What kind of sin did John and his readers consider mortal? Much has been written about what sins are, and are not, "mortal." Since John does not elaborate at this point, it is likely he had in mind the issues of belief that Jesus came in the flesh, obedience to God, and love, which are foci of his letter. Though interpretation is difficult, we would maintain that mortal sins were failures in these areas, coupled with an impenitent spirit. Though not forbidding it, John did not counsel prayer for such hardened cases.

In view of sins not mortal, what kind of prayers were to be prayed, especially keeping in mind what we have said previously regarding free will? Could not such a sinner pray for his or her own sins to be forgiven? Why were the prayers of others necessary? The context (v. 14) indicates that prayers are to be according to God's will. Sins that were not mortal may not be so strange to us for they may well be those of which we are guilty every day. In this particular context, they may involve failures in the practices of love and of obedience to God. We assume these were the sins of those whose deepest desire was to serve God, but who failed at certain points.

On this basis, we believe John's concerns were the same as those of the rest of the New Testament—prayers for the spiritual welfare of fellow Christians. Certainly Christians can pray for the forgiveness of their own sins. Yet human psychology is such that we long for the prayers of others. We feel a sense of shame in asking God to forgive. We also have an awareness of our own weakness—a weakness we would be glad to have overcome by the strength of others. And we also just want to know that others care enough to intercede on our behalf.

In consonance with free will, we must repeat that God's gift of forgiveness is not forced upon those unwilling to receive it. But for tender souls seeking purification, intercessory prayer can offer powerful ministry.

### PRAYERS FOR DELIVERANCE FROM OPPRESSION

These prayers are discussed above, where I argued that it was not physical safety that was of primary concern, but rather the ability to continue preaching the gospel.

- Acts 12:5, 12. The church was praying for Peter, who was imprisoned and likely facing death. The content of the prayer is not given, but it may have been for God to strengthen Peter in his ordeal, though likely it was also for Peter's release, as subsequent events indicated.

- Romans 15:31. Paul asked Christians to pray that he would be delivered from unbelievers in Judea. When we read of the mob that seized and nearly killed Paul in Jerusalem before his rescue by Roman soldiers (Acts 21:35–36), we see why he was concerned. He faced considerable trauma, but he was eventually delivered, and in spite of all hazards that seemed to make his planned journey to Rome a failure, we see him at the end of Acts preaching openly and unhindered in the Imperial City.

- 2 Corinthians 1:11. Paul asked for intercessory prayers for deliverance from an unspecified danger.

- Philippians 1:19. Paul expressed confidence that through the prayers of the Philippians and the help of the Spirit, he would be delivered as he endured his imprisonment.

- 2 Thessalonians 3:2. Here Paul requested that the Thessalonians pray that he would be delivered from wicked and evil men so that God's word would be fully proclaimed. Paul wrote these words from Corinth. In that wicked city, he had cause to fear such opposition. However, Acts 18:9–10 records a vision given him of the risen Lord in which he was reassured that no one would attack and harm him. One wonders what connection there was between the prayers of the Thessalonians and the vision.

### PRAYERS FOR CHILDREN

- Matthew 19:13. Where the parallels in Mark 10:13 and Luke 18:15 say children were brought to Jesus so he could touch them, Matthew says they were brought so Jesus could pray for them. This was probably a desire for a teacher to bless children. So far as the rest of the New Testament is concerned, there is no later reference to this practice, and it is not modeled as a practice in the early church. Nonetheless, these texts may signal to parents and friends the importance of prayer for those younger so that, in every way, they can be given powerful leading in the ways of God.

## PRAYERS FOR THOSE WITH SPECIAL SPIRITUAL RESPONSIBILITY

- Acts 6:6. The seven selected to deal with the problem of division over provision for the widows were set before the apostles, who prayed and laid hands upon them. This would be a commissioning, an investiture with the authority of the apostles, and a call for the wisdom and power of God to enable their ministry. The repeated references to the Spirit (vv. 3, 5) indicate how strongly the church recognized the need for divine blessings and empowerment as this delicate problem was resolved. The next verse (v. 7), in detailing further evangelistic success, is testimony to the working of God in using the seven to repair the potential breach in the body.

- Acts 13:3. Just as the power of the Spirit and prayer were crucial in Acts 6, the case is the same here. The missionaries, Barnabas and Saul, were set apart at the Spirit's direction and sent out after fasting and praying by the church and its leaders. The events of this tour (chapters 13, 14) in producing conversions, in dealing with hardship, and in strengthening the infant congregations, testify to the need for and results of prayer in these activities.

- Acts 14:23. When Paul and Barnabas, at some risk, returned to churches previously founded on their first tour, they offered warnings and encouragements. They also appointed elders in every church, and "with prayer and fasting . . . committed them to the Lord."

In these last three texts, we see three kinds of responsibility in Christian activity: the ministry of reconciliation (Acts 6), evangelism (Acts 13—cf. chapter 8 of this book), and spiritual oversight (Acts 14). These are heavy callings, with the potential of producing great good. When one considers the day-to-day details these tasks involved (we are given a glimpse in Paul's first tour), the need for divine empowerment can be appreciated more fully. Certainly those in similar roles today readily can sense how necessary prayer is in their ministries. Those in the church need constantly to aid these leaders with prayer. The success or failure of God's work, humanly speaking, depends on the quality of the leadership in that work. Leaders have a tremendous need for wisdom. The challenges of special tasks can be quite wearing, so they have a great need for inner peace and calm. We need to remember, as well, that prayers for those with special responsibility have an effect on our own lives, as those ministers work for our spiritual betterment.

As we review the passages discussed in this chapter, we see that most are for "inside prayers" rather than for "outside prayers." By "inside prayers," we mean prayers for God to work in the hearts and minds of believers. Since believers want to grow to be more like Christ, there is a joining of the nature of the intercession with the heart of the one for whom intercession was made. Then, as hearts are blessed, the work of God, flowing from such hearts, will be more powerfully carried out.

"Outside prayers" are those asking God to alter circumstances external to the heart. Such prayers are rare in the New Testament, if found at all. The only prayers of intercession that could come in this category would be those for physical safety. Yet even these could be understood in ways that really see them as "inside prayers."

Since the New Testament evidence is so scanty, it is hard to know how God is expected to change matters. People who expect miracles like those wrought in the New Testament tend to interpret favorable events as miraculous. Others of deep faith look at the same events and see them as part of the natural process, though they do not deny the intervention of God in the process. I have even known of occasions where one Christian interpreted an event as being the hand of God, while another Christian interpreted the same event as being satanic in origin. My personal conviction is that God is powerfully active in response to our prayers but that his intervention *appears* to us as part of a natural process. Thus these results are open to different interpretations, depending on the theology of the interpreter. I like to call these divine responses *providence*, by which

I mean those things done by God in answer to prayer that appear natural as viewed by humans. These events are interpreted as God's deeds by our faith in prayer and in God's answering power.

All this is shrouded in mystery. God is active in our world, but we have difficulty in explaining how. When we have made all our analyses, we still must recognize that God's actions never can be completely captured by our systems and outlines. We do our best to be biblical in our understanding, and then bow in humility.

These following conclusions will summarize what I have been stressing:

First, I am convinced that intercessory prayer should never be understood in a way that denies human freedom of choice. Still, we must recognize that God may work in ways that would lead persons to arrive at certain conclusions as they pray for guidance in making choices. We think of this especially in connection with evangelism. God may use the pray-er in an especially convincing way. Personal contacts may be more than accidental and may have an influence. Perhaps other circumstances can influence the way the prayed-for person thinks. One should certainly pray for wisdom in this process—what to do and say, and when.

Second, intercessory prayer is effective when the one who is the object of prayer desires that for which the intercessor is praying. Third, prayers should be offered within biblical parameters. It is true that the New Testament cannot, or does not, explicitly detail everything that might be requested. But the larger principles of Scripture always offer a framework within which all prayers should be considered. God will certainly answer a prayer for Christians to be more loving. But he does not promise to answer prayers to win the lottery, nor does he even authorize such prayers. When we pray for something we are not sure about (since we do not possess the wisdom to always know what is best), we might do well to lay the case before God, tell him what we believe is best and why, and then ask, in humility, that his will be done.

Let us conclude by noting ways in which we see the great value of intercessory prayer.

1. These prayers both demonstrate and promote the love that binds Christians together. Christians have a special desire to do good to one another, and these prayers are reflections of that. Again and again, we have observed Christians experience such

deep life concerns that they are shaken to their very foundations. It is enormous comfort in such times to know that our concern is joined by the concern of other believers who are linked with us in prayer. The thanks we offer those who pray for us at such times comes from the deepest places in our hearts. We sing a hymn that speaks of sorrow that goes from eye to eye and joy from heart to heart, and these beautiful words indicate how in the Christian faith, God helps us to be truly sensitive to the needs of others, as reflected in our intercessory prayers.

2. We have pondered the relation of God's answers to our faith and fervency in prayer. Intellectual problems aside, we feel impelled, in times of great need, to implore others to join us in prayer. If God's response is in some way proportionate to our faith and fervency in asking, it would seem to follow that many people praying would be more potent than one person praying alone. Even if the prayers of many are no more significant than the prayers of one person, we are still comforted by the prayers of others. Yet in some way, we want to see a greater power in collective prayers, even if we cannot fully explain why. I spoke earlier of a dear friend who contracted a life-threatening form of cancer. In his extremity, he called on many Christian friends to join him in a covenant of prayer. Today he is free of the disease. We like to think it was the massed prayers of God's people that had an effect in his case. Whatever the situation, what this friend did in calling for prayers was right and is what any of us is likely do in similar circumstances.

3. Sometimes we do not recognize our real needs. We turn to others who may have a clearer vision and ask for their prayers. Such intercessory prayer is a good antidote to blind spots.

4. There are times in life when we know we need prayer, but for whatever reason, we have hit a dry season. Then in our weakness, we turn to Christian friends and ask them to do for us what we feel we cannot do for ourselves. Perhaps this was the case with Simon the sorcerer. Thus, one Christian's weakness can be shored up by another's strength.

5. When we ask others to pray for us, we recognize that life really can be dealt with only when our concerns are laid at God's feet. Humans are too inclined to think they know better what they need than God does. Requesting prayer acknowledges confidence in God's governance of the world and of our lives. It engenders humility because we must recognize our weakness and lack of wisdom.

We have explored various facets of the prayer of intercession. But prayer is much more than a doctrine to be studied. If it is no more than that, it is really nothing. Prayer is a thing to be done, for God does hear and answer. We must believe this to become the church victorious. The challenge of the hour and of all life is to have such a loving regard for other men, and such a faith in the power of God, that we commit our lives to a fervent ministry of prayer, including sincere intercession for others.

## Thoughts to Ponder

1. How are we to pray for our enemies? For what should we pray?

2. How do you understand John 5:16?

3. How can we offer intercessory prayers for non-Christians?

4. How can we do the same for children? What of blessings for children?

5. Discuss the viability, in Scripture, of "inside prayers" and "outside prayers."

6. What of those who are prone to interpret outside events as answers to prayer?

7. What is your opinion about "providence"?

# CHAPTER SIXTEEN

# HOW CAN WE KNOW HOW OUR PRAYERS ARE ANSWERED?

Recently the church to which I minister was giving serious thought to the support of missionaries. The available funds were limited and there were more candidates asking for support than we could help. To complicate the problem all of those requesting assistance were persons of high quality and ability. All parties concerned prayed intensively throughout the long period of evaluation, and when the final decision was made it was assumed that God's hand had somehow directed the decision.

This is just one example among similar situations that occur all the time. Churches pray for guidance in many aspects of their work and with regard to their staffing. Young people pray about where to attend school and whom to marry. Prayers are offered with regard to geographical locations, jobs, and life directions. You could add your own concrete situation to this more general list. When we must make choices, and the options do not give black and white guidance, how are we to know what God wants of us? And the task is complicated by those among us who seem so sure of God's guidance and who speak unhesitatingly of how and where God is leading them. Not all of us feel quite this decisive.

A further complication arises when those decisions about which people were so sure turn out to be bad decisions. The marriage ended in a tragic divorce; the missionary returned from the field with a broken spirit; the job was not what it promised to be. How are we to understand this? Did God give bad answers? Perhaps people interpreted something as God's answer that was not his answer at all but that was only their *wants*, which they subconsciously elevated to the place of divine guidance. How can we know? How can we keep from being deceived, from deceiving ourselves?

However we find answers to these issues, Scripture must be our guide. Since prayers about major life decisions are so significant, we often become quite emotionally involved in seeking answers, and these feelings can easily lead us to views that are not biblical but that we would like to invest with biblical authority. It is a strict course to run, staying with the Scriptures, but it is the way we must go; we must not allow our feet to wander out of the ways God has opened before us.

## When the Answer Is Clear

There are many prayers we can pray where God's answer will be quite clear. When we pray for a specific aspect of Christian growth and see ourselves growing as we pray, we can know God has answered. When we pray for our marriages and see them blessed as we have asked, we can know. When we ask for deeper understanding and more effective application of the truths of Christianity and are given them, we can know. When we pray to resist temptation and the strength is given, we can know. When we pray for God to open doors so that we can render service and he does, we can know. Over the years, I have heard numerous stories from those who have prayed for God to give them blessings of this sort and have received as God has promised. Some of these changes, given by God in response to fervent, even desperate, prayers, have been of a sort the person praying had never experienced before. Some, God helped completely turn from lifelong wrong habits and attitudes. I have known others who were nearly paralyzed by fear on the eve of major surgeries that had potentially disastrous consequences. Through prayer, they found a calm they never dreamed could be theirs, the peace that passes understanding.

I recall a personal experience, many years ago, in which I was called half a nation away to appear before an angry group of accusers who thought wrongly that I was denying the authority of Scripture. The trip to that "trial" was comprised of large amounts of both fear and prayer. The prayers were answered, however, in a marvelous way. When the time came for confrontation, God blessed me with an inner repose that still amazes me today. My fears had been colossal, but God's power over-topped my fears, subdued them, and replaced them with his powerful peace. I absolutely could not have gone through the experience so calmly by my own resources.

## WHEN THE ANSWER IS NOT CLEAR

When we see the results for which we have prayed, we can know God has answered. But such prayers are not the problematic requests for guidance for God to show us what decisions to make, where to go, or what relationships to form. We turn again to the New Testament for enlightenment but this time the trip to the well yields little. There is the case in Acts 1:15–26 where the disciples prayed regarding the replacement for Judas. But it seems obvious the subtext there was some sort of divine instruction to name a replacement. The casting of lots makes the most sense if we assume that God directed how the lots fell. When we try to bring this text into our world and make application, we find we are missing the kind of divine influence that must have operated there. Yet any decision we make should have as a primary concern the relation of that decision to our Christian faith and life.

So, how do *we* discern God's answer when our prayerful minds envision more than one possibility and we must make decisions? How can we know how God is leading us? Or if he is giving us any direction at all, save the call to be his child, whatever or wherever? How can we avoid being self-deceived, or even being led astray by the Tempter? Let me suggest three possible answers to this dilemma, one of which I personally reject, and two of which I believe carry validity:

1. Some good people believe God will grace them with a direct revelation, delivered in some form not perceptible to other people. But whenever I hear such claims, certain concerns come

to my mind. I remember the story of the young prophet out of Judah (1 Kings 13) who got into trouble and eventually lost his life because he believed an older prophet who told him that he had received a revelation countermanding the one God had earlier delivered to the young prophet.

When I am told by some Christians of a revelation by which God directed them in a decision, I wonder why they received such direct divine guidance when I and millions of others have not? Not that I consider myself more worthy. But what divine logic works this way with some people and not with others? Then, if this "direct divine advice" turns out badly, I wonder if the source was really God, after all? Would he lead people into tragic situations?

I wonder, too, at the credentials of those claiming this direct guidance. Is their Christian walk so spiritual, so intimately in tune with God, that we should expect them to receive such direct communication? Does their life so fully manifest Christ's service ethic that they would be readily recognized as spiritual giants, even without their claims of revelations? Or do the declarations of direct input from God sound more like bragging than anything else? We must be very careful in deciding what God will or will not do.

2. A second approach to the issue holds that God answers the prayer for guidance but through indirect means. As we pray, we consider all we know about Christianity and the ways it could impact our decisions. As we ponder the possibilities, we allow ourselves to be guided by our best and wisest reflections. We may also find help by reading the Scriptures or by reading other Christian materials. It is even possible that valid insights may surface through secular reading. Conversations with others, especially with wise and respected advisers, can be beneficial. Circumstances may condition how we decide. Doors may open that were closed when we began praying, or contrarily, doors may close that were once open. There are so many ways God may work to answer prayers that we cannot imagine them all.

As we proceed along this line of this thinking, we must constantly ask certain questions. Which course would be the most loving? Where would our stewardship best be discharged? In which situation would we develop most effectively into the image of Christ? Where could we best be the kind of servants Jesus calls us to be? Are we pursuing a given possibility for material or egotistical benefits, or for Christian reasons? Which decision most fully works for the glory of God? What is the path of greatest wisdom? These are not easy issues to resolve, but we can pray for insight.

If the decision we must make is bound to a deadline, when the time comes, we must decide on the basis of those factors noted above, as well as by any others that arrest our attention, and then we must believe the decision we make is the one to which we are being guided.

There is a great danger in this, or any, process by which we attempt to determine God's direction. We have suggested before, and must reiterate, that it is always possible that we could allow our wants to intrude into the process so strongly that we do not "hear" God. But the opposite is also a danger—we might reject a course because it also satisfies our likings—we are afraid of liking it too much. God may, after all, lead us where we make more money, achieve greater advancement, enroll in a school we truly enjoy, or marry a person who makes us phenomenally happy. We should not assume that God desires us to be either poor or rich (to use a material illustration to stand for any of several possibilities); he may take us any direction he sees fit. We can be either too selfish or too self-negating. These dangers suggest another important aspect of our prayers. We should ask God for the gift of openness and honesty, for preservation from being self-deceived.

3. There is a third way to approach this matter. I do not believe it applies in every case, but it may be the case with some. It assumes that the decision God really wants us to make is to live according to his will as it is revealed in Scripture and that he may not give any specific guidance. After all our prayers and considerations, we still may not find any leading. Nonetheless, in such cases, we still must rely heavily on prayer. God is saying, "Go either way you want. Both are acceptable. The important thing is

that you believe and live as I have called you to do." Taking this view relieves us of the worrisome responsibility of having to find an answer when there may not be one to find. Often I hear people who, when asked about their plans, say, "I am just waiting for the Lord to show me the way." This trust in God is admirable, but we must not use a passive posture to ignore personal enterprise. Further, we must hold ourselves open to the possibility that no clear option may present itself, yet we must make the decision.

Often we hear it said that God may give one of three possible answers to prayers. One is "yes," a second "no," and a third "wait a while." But not every situation yields itself easily to this formula. Sometimes our perception of the answer may be "I don't know." If the time comes, when we must act we proceed by doing what we do know from Scripture. Perhaps subsequent events will offer further insight. If not, then we accept what we have done. We may live all of our lives to God's glory on the basis of actions taken when "we don't know."

Here is my great fear as I write these words: I do not want them to be understood as mere intellectualizing. Above all, we should lay all aspects of our lives before God. He should always be our major partner in making decisions. He does expect us to use the minds he has given us and to evaluate options in terms of his revelation. But even more, he wishes us to make every move conscious that he is Lord of our lives. If you draw only one lesson from this chapter, I hope you will see how important it is to pray about all the concerns of our lives.

## Thoughts to Ponder

1. How can our feelings and desires deceive us with regard to God's answers to prayer?

2. What does the New Testament teach about how God answers prayers for direction and guidance? Are our views on this subject biblical?

3.  Some would argue that they receive direct guidance from God in answer to prayers for guidance. Is it possible this could be a sign of a weak faith, rather than a strong faith? Discuss.

4.  Just how will God guide us? Do we have all the guidance we need in Scripture? Isn't this all of God's will that is necessary?

# Chapter Seventeen

# Public Prayers

Early in my Christian experience, when I was in my late teens, I tended to be somewhat dogmatic in my religious pronouncements. A member of my family, likely weary of my inflexibility, asked if we had public prayers where I attended church. When I replied in the affirmative, I was asked how I could reconcile that practice with Jesus' instructions to pray secretly, in one's closet (Matt. 6:6). How could I claim "my church" went strictly by the Bible, when our public prayers seemed to be such a flagrant disregard of Scripture? Caught out and desperate, I fled to my minister with this dilemma. He pointed out that Scripture gives instances of both public and private prayer. The text in Matthew, I learned upon further observation, addressed the hypocrisy of showy public prayers uttered to impress others, not the normal prayers spoken in church, though they certainly are not exempt from this flaw.

For many people, public prayers constitute a larger part of their prayer lives than do private ones. In some religious contexts, these prayers are written in advance, and the congregation or the leader reads them aloud. In other places, the prayers are presented as spontaneous, though these still are often delivered after forethought. In both kinds of prayer, the danger is that the congregation may not truly pray the prayer, due to inattention, lack of comprehension, theological objections, or other considerations. In this chapter, we will discuss public prayers with its goals and intents, and with a view to its effectiveness, both on the part of the leader and on the part of those led.

## PUBLIC PRAYER IN THE NEW TESTAMENT

There is a fair amount of New Testament evidence describing the corporate prayers of the early believers. The apostles, with Jesus' brothers, his mother and other women, prayed as they gathered after the Lord's ascension (Acts 1:14). Later, the group who prayed as they selected a successor for Judas was about 120 strong (Acts 1:24ff.). The apostles prayed together in connection with the selection of the seven men who were dedicated to seeing the Jerusalem widows were cared for so that the division in the church would be healed (Acts 6:6). Christians gathered at Mary's house to pray for the imprisoned Peter (Acts 12:5, 12). The church in Antioch of Syria prayed as they sent Barnabas and Saul forth as missionaries (Acts 13:3). Paul prayed with the Ephesian elders (Acts 20:26) and with Christian friends from Tyre (Acts 21:5). He also gave thanks for food with the crew on board the storm-wracked ship carrying him to Rome (Acts 27:35). This last case duplicates the many times Jesus himself had prayed publicly at meals (feeding the five thousand, feeding the four thousand, the Last Supper, and on the road to Emmaus with two disciples). In addition to these references, the Lord's Prayer no doubt implies a public gathering, since Matthew's account speaks of "our" Father (Matt. 6:9).

In 1 Corinthians, Paul addressed issues of public prayers because of abuses that needed to be corrected (see 11:4–9, 13; and 14:13–19). The reference to saying "amen," or "so be it," in 1 Corinthians 14:16 denotes a communal assent given to prayer. It had the effect of personalizing the prayer.

## ASSUMPTIONS AND BENEFITS

The assumption behind the prayers within the early Christian community was the recognition of a common mind. The meal prayers, prayed when both believers and unbelievers were present, bore witness to God's gracious provision of life's necessities. Public prayer has been, and should be, significant in the life of the church. Unfortunately it often becomes a ritual, done out of obligation. I suspect many Christians, though they comport themselves respectfully during such prayers, have all but given up on considering them effective avenues of approach to God. Minds wander, people make evaluations of the prayer, and the slightest detractions carry one away from the event, so that the closing "amen" simply calls people back to the matters at hand.

But the nature of prayer and the needs of the church compel us to attend to these public petitions so they can be powerfully effective as God intends they should. Since we often utter these prayers when we are together, they should mean something, lest we be characterized by inattention, or worse, by hypocrisy. As the church, we do well to add a vocal "amen" at the conclusion of public prayers, but how can this be a significant word for us as "listeners" if we have not prayed the prayer ourselves?

Consider the following: We are a people called out and called together, and one of our identifying marks is our conviction that God's power is operating in our lives (cf. Acts 2:42). We tend to be more sensitive to this as individuals, but we also need to be aware of God's involvement as we in the church consider our common goals, needs, concerns, and view of life. Corporate prayers remind us of who we are. It is easy for any of us to so dedicate ourselves to certain aspects of the faith (evangelism, corporate worship, benevolence, and so on), that other important Christianity elements recede from our view. Group prayer can restore balance and can remind us of what might have slipped away.

In our chapter on intercessory prayer, we observed how helpful it is to have others praying for us when our own prayer lives are weak. Public prayer can be a solidifying and bonding experience for our times of instability. Such prayer certainly may be the stimulus to a more vigorous private prayer life as well.

When we pray together, we recognize our need for each other. Such prayers affirm our nature as a community bound by a special love. We are partners in a great enterprise, players on the same team, soldiers shoulder to shoulder in the greatest of battles. It can be a time that provokes the strongest appreciation of those whose lives are cast with our lives in God's service.

Of what do these prayers consist? Certainly prayers of thanks and adoration are particularly appropriate here. We are grateful, and public prayers can spark and stimulate these appreciations in our lives. We also lift individuals before God as they experience various life crises and ask that God's love may be palpable and powerful in granting healing to them. At the same time, we ask God to use us as ministers of his love, peace, and joy in service to our brethren and to others. There are common tasks for which we pray, and we ask God to bless those who have special responsibilities (including elders, ministers, staff persons, teachers, and deacons). Every congregation must select its priorities in ministry, and every congregation needs wisdom and power in its service for the Lord, so these constitute pressing prayer needs. Any readers who reflect on these words in relation to a particular church can think of many specific prayers and needs in their own contexts.

We may struggle to analyze the dynamics of corporate action. We can see prayer power at work in many ways, but we are not sure just why many people praying together has particular efficacy. Yet we believe it does, and the church continues to pray, confident that as we do so, special things happen through God's grace. We assume there are qualities of a "we" activity that do not characterize an "I" activity.

Many Christians can testify to the power and excitement of public prayers in their experiences. But unfortunately, this positive experience is not universal. Some of us have frequently found public prayer more dulling than edifying. When communion with God should be the goal, the best we can manage may be a quiet respect during the interval between "Our Father" and "amen." Sometimes, we even fail in demonstrating true respect and find ourselves either mentally criticizing the prayer or taking a mental leave of absence from the public prayer time. Though we may berate ourselves for not being fully involved in the prayer, there is something to be said for a lovingly critical attitude that aims to resolve problems that may burden our public prayers. It is in desiring to help our prayers, not to detract from them, that I offer the following considerations of possible problems, because I believe that strengthening our public prayers will strengthen our fellowships.

Have you ever made the effort to focus on the words of a prayer leader, doing your best to make his or her words your prayer, when some statement brought you up short, and you thought, "I can't pray that"? Has the wording of public prayer ever been such that you were excluded from the praying group? If so, read on.

## HINDRANCES TO EFFECTIVE PUBLIC PRAYER

1. The problem of "unsound" teaching. I know it is easy to take extreme positions with regard to "orthodox" expressions of Christian belief. I know, too, that when immature Christians lead public prayers, they may utter theological inaccuracies simply because their grasp of the faith is quite incomplete. Nonetheless, if I hear a prayer leader make statements that are severely wrong regarding the nature of God, Christ, or the Spirit, my mind pauses. Likewise when I hear prayers demanding that God act in a certain way when God himself has not told us what he might do. I am sure you can make your own list of similar concerns. When I come to these moments, I fear I become an evaluator of theological orthodoxy rather than a part of the praying community. I don't want to let concern for doctrinal correctness overcome personal dedication, but it is important to understand Christianity aright, and that is no less true in our prayers than elsewhere.

2. The problem of affectations and distracting habits. If the person leading prayer deliberately or inadvertently draws primary attention to himself or herself, then the focus of the audience is directed to the wrong place. Our attention should be on God and, sometimes, on the God-man relationship. Think about the following: What of the person who sees prayer as a performance, who uses the performance as a stage from which to impress? Praying before a large audience at a lectureship, conference, workshop, or seminar, the guilty party may think such eloquence could lead to speaking invitations or other opportunities. It is easy, at times, to forget what Jesus said about not praying to impress men. He observed that such prayers certainly could accomplish that goal, but, alas, they would not be heard by the Father (Matt. 6:5–6).

One admires a well-crafted prayer. But it is possible that such a prayer may be more a work of art than communication with the Lord. On one occasion, after hearing such a prayer, a friend and I wondered together if such beauty of language was necessary to carry the message, whether the prayer was any more effective because of it. Of course, we do not want lazy, slovenly prayers, but the opposite extreme of trying to compose a masterpiece of wording also has its drawbacks. It may be true that God is due the best we can give, whether it be in the literary quality of a prayer or something else, but prayer is a means of communicating with God, not art for art's sake.

Other distracting qualities have nothing to do with showiness but are rather due to inexperience or fear. I think of the earnest leader, often a young person, who overuses the words "just" and "really" as a way of expressing sincerity. Then there is what I call the "petitionary sigh," a deep breath drawn and exhaled as the prayer is begun, and sometimes at intervals in the prayer. These, I suspect, are intended to reflect the awesomeness of addressing the Creator. Such awe is profoundly right, but the accompanying "breathiness" often detracts from the prayer. Another distraction is the insertion of "Father" or "Lord" into the text of the prayer with an unnecessary frequency. Some hearers, with a certain sense of shame, have actually counted these "insertions" in prayers they have heard. The total is often quite amazing.

These are not "big" things, and they may only be disturbing to people of a certain turn of mind, but we should consider them if they detract from the powerful thing that public prayer can be. I suspect many prayer leaders are not even aware of what they are doing, and with a bit of attention and forethought, they could alleviate the problem.

3. Another distraction is the use of trite and overworked language. Of course I know of the power of tradition and sameness in reenforcing those things about which we need to be reminded. That is why we celebrate Communion every week. But I am thinking of overused formulae that may demonstrate lack of thought in prayer, phrases that are so familiar they slip past us without any sense of meaning, simply because we have heard them too often. I once heard an entire sermon in which I knew every statement beforehand, because the verbiage was so overused. Some prayers suffer from the same problem.

We also face the problem of burdensome repetition. Who can say how many times in a single prayer a certain word or phrase (such as "petition," "thanks," or "come before") should be repeated? Not even once is necessary when we consider that God knows our hearts before we even express ourselves. But since the prayer is public, one time is necessary. But are any more needed? Do we think God did not get the message the first time? No one intends to insult God by reminding him again, so why do it?

I am not deeming any such prayers as insincere. The leader may be experiencing stage fright, turning his mouth on and his mind off out of panic. Nor do I necessarily deny the truthfulness of the overused expressions. But I suspect that in at least some cases, the smooth flow of overly familiar words constitutes an easy performance that does not take prayer seriously. How do you react to expressions like, "all wise and ever to be adored Heavenly Father," "we thank thee for all material and especially all spiritual blessings," or "guard, guide, and protect"? I am sure many readers could extend this list with their own most-familiar phrases. I do not wish to be unduly harsh, but I believe that devoting more thought and attention to the uttering of public prayers might lead to some helpful modification.

4. I have known of several instances where a warning was given that "brother X" should not be asked to lead, since he "thinks prayers must be eternal to be immortal." Occasionally I have sat or stood with head bowed and eyes closed for what seemed an eternity. I am not objecting to prayers that truly need to be long, but in this case, the leader, having gone once through his "list" of prayer topics, felt it necessary to go round that way again. Lord, forgive us our intemperate thoughts on such occasions.

5. I admit there are times when it is appropriate for a prayer to impart information, for the sake of clarity or edification, or to comfort or show concern. I can hardly see how providing information for the benefit of other people present can be criticized.

Some prayers, however, seem to assume God will not know certain things if *we* do not inform *him*. In my world, I often see this happen in public prayers for the sick. Prior to praying, the leader asks for prayer needs, and those present share their concerns. Yet even though the group members have just given the context of their requests, once in prayer, the leader feels the need to editorialize. God knows the needs—they have just been announced—and neither repetition nor editorializing is necessary for the effectiveness of the prayer. The editorial comments add nothing, and sometimes are (if I may say it) somewhat inane.

6. Some use prayer as a vehicle to preach, especially where others might not be willing to listen otherwise. When we are in the attentive and reverential mode called for by prayer, we suffer an abuse of the situation when we are compelled to hear a homily. The practice of preaching through prayer turns the experience from one addressed to God to one addressed to man. One would almost expect such a prayer to conclude with, "Amen. Now let us stand and sing the song of invitation." Prayer is prayer, and a sermon is a sermon. Is disguising a sermon as a prayer completely honest? Might it not cause resentment on the part of the hearers and engender hostility, rather than openness, to the message preached?

I once attended a small chapel service at a Christian school, and a professor of political science was asked to lead the prayer. He began appropriately enough, but ere long had diverted his comments into asking God to bless aspects of his own political program, which involved interpretations of certain national and international affairs and implied criticisms of leaders with whom he disagreed. His concerns may or may not have been just and holy, but they certainly were not shared by all present, so his could not be a community prayer. No wonder the aftermath was not satisfaction at the wonder of corporate prayer—instead, debate ensued. The group's focus was turned to the one praying rather than to God.

Abuses like this one can be theological, not just political. I once heard a story of a preacher who was invited to give the invocation at the meeting of a civic club, composed of community members of various religious and nonreligious persuasions. Because he was a man of strong convictions, and because he saw an opportunity to tell those there what they would not listen to him say otherwise, he bowed his head and preached a thirty-minute sermon on a point of doctrine that he deemed biblical but with which certain of his listeners would disagree. I am sure that plenty of audience members felt that the preacher had taken unfair advantage of them.

7. In ancient days (and, I presume, in the Psalms), communal prayers were sometimes expressed using first person singular pronouns. I realize that even today, on occasion a prayer leader may say "I " and mean "we." I certainly can take part in such a prayer. But at other times, the one leading public prayer prays in private ways, where the "I" is only him or her. When I hear such a prayer, I feel excluded. The leader's concern is not mine. Such exclusion, I feel, is inappropriate. It is important for prayer leaders to give careful forethought to the concerns of the community they are leading and use judgment in expressing purely personal concerns in public forums. After all, the congregation cannot give a truthful "amen" to a prayer that is not theirs.

8. Last, for the entire group to give assent to a prayer, each person must understand what is prayed. Imprecise allusions, unclear vocabulary or language usages, or confusing expressions can deny a prayer its true purposes. I once heard a prayer at a Communion service that was so garbled and bewildering that, if it fit the occasion at all, it was beyond me to know how, or even to know what was said. In that case, the mystery became tragically clear when it was revealed that the person praying was intoxicated, but then, I have also heard confounding prayers from those who were stone sober.

We find a biblical instance supporting this point is discovered in 1 Corinthians 14:14–18 where Paul wrote of the misuse of the gift of tongues in the assembly. Without an interpreter, he said, prayer in tongues would be meaningless, and the congregation could give no "amen" to such a prayer. He indicated that one should pray with the mind as well as with the spirit. In other words, the prayer should not be obscure to those who hear it.

## How to Pray: Leaders and Listeners

The experience of leading a group in prayer is one to be taken seriously. Those whose private prayer lives are powerful may be able to lead spontaneous public prayers in an effective way, but I suspect this responsibility is best discharged with forethought about what the nature of the experience should be and how to express what one best knows to be the mind of the group. In practicality, public prayer may need to be more generalized in contrast to the more personal elements in private expressions. But certainly the one leading public prayer should have a deep faith in the efficacy of prayer and choose his or her words accordingly. Without such a commitment, one would do better to decline to lead than simply to go through a performance.

Public prayer will express the particular needs and concerns of the praying community, but the leaders should also take a global view. The whole gamut of temptations, needs, virtues, and empowerments should be kept in mind, for all of these issues are to be found among those who join in the prayer. For example, the meanings and applications of praying "hallowed be thy name" will vary from person to person as the words are spoken. Without the advantage of being individually specific, a corporate prayer should offer a field inside of which each person's circumstances could be fit. There may also be times when public prayers, in response to individual requests, may be very specific in what they ask. The entire congregation wants to unite in praying for those asking for intercession in their marital difficulties, employment problems, or decision-making challenges. These prayers are appropriate as evidence of the love and concern Christians bear for one another.

Those who silently follow the prayer leader must try to shut out distractions, which is one benefit of closing one's eyes. Some find it useful to express a silent or quiet "amen" to each part of the prayer. Following a leader certainly demands focus and concentration, we will do better if we recognize that it is our prayer, not just a prayer belonging to the leader.

## Striving toward the Goal

Has this chapter, in speaking of problems of public prayer, been too picky? Is God going to refuse us when prayers are not entirely correct?

I think not. Truth to tell, prayer leaders may often fall short of leading the ideal public prayer for various reasons. But with due regard for a loving and understanding God, I want to hold my ground. Is the church to settle for mediocrity on the ground that the pursuit of perfection is too demanding? I do not think so. We know we do not pray as we ought, and we may never reach the goal of perfect prayer. But God's gift should be used in God's way, to achieve his purposes. We should never slack in moving toward the goal of excellence. Great artists do not settle for sloppy work, for that is not how masterpieces are created, whether in painting, sculpture, symphonies, or novels. When we look upon Jesus and what he did for us, how can we respond to him with less than our best? After all, the sacrifices in Israel demanded animals without blemish, and Malachi scored the people of his day for insulting God by offering him blind, lame, or sick animals (Mal. 1:8). The principle is clear. God should have the best we can offer. Though we are never at our absolute best or perfectly in line with the ideal, we continue moving toward the goal, to the greater glory of God.

## BE BOLD

Now, a practical word. I imagine myself teaching a lesson in a church context in which I would point out the problems often faced in public prayer. Someone in the meeting has been asked to lead prayer after my talk and is so intimidated by what we have just discussed that he feels like he is dodging hazards in an obstacle course in even attempting to pray. If I have left the impression that public prayer is largely structured in terms of what not to do, then I have not done what I intended. I am not asking about what God will or will not hear, for he is aware of all our prayers. We should pray away, not fearful that we will make a mistake, but continually thinking about and striving to improve what we do. I am still haunted by an experience that happened many years ago. In the congregation where I preached, a new Christian was asked to lead a prayer at Communion. He agreed, and he prayed quite well. Afterward, he said to me, "I hope I didn't say anything wrong." What have I done to this man, I thought, that he sees prayer as an activity in which he fears any misstep? I don't want this chapter to have a similar effect on any readers, but I do want to challenge us to a more powerful life of public prayer.

## Thoughts to Ponder

1. How can we solve the problem of inattention during public prayer?

2. What should be the basic content concerns in public prayer?

3. Why should we have public prayer? Why shouldn't private prayers be sufficient?

4. How do you react to the distracting qualities of a prayer leader indicated in this chapter?

# QUESTIONS AND ANSWERS

The main emphasis of this book has been to construct a New Testament theology of prayer. But many questions that surface about the practice of prayer are not directly addressed in Scripture. In these final pages, we will be considering some of these questions. I will consider relevant biblical texts as much as possible and will try to base all I say on the larger sense of Scripture. Some of what is said will be my own opinions. I hope they will be right, but I know my insights may sometimes be lacking. I invite readers to produce their own resolutions to these questions while adhering to what guidance Scripture offers. If you disagree with me, perhaps I can learn from you.

*1—Just what is a prayer?*

People pray in many ways, as we have noted previously in this book. Some are formally composed before delivery. Some are structured in formal liturgies; others are free, expository prayers, composed on the spot (though often with significant consideration in advance). There are private prayers, prayers in large assemblies, and prayers in small groups. Some prayers are audible, and some are silent. Some authors even speak of prayer without words. Some prayers are made during special devotional times, and others are prayed during the course of a day or night. Some Christians speak of a stream-of-consciousness prayer life that goes on continually in their hearts. Sometimes when someone asks us to pray for them, or when we volunteer such prayers, that in itself may be a form of prayer. When we think in a Godwards way of those in need, may that not also be a prayer? If one is a Christian and sees all life through the lens of the relation to God, might not much of that life also be a prayer?

Sometimes we tend to think the only prayers that "count" are those expressed during a deliberately specified prayer time; some people do not think hearing public prayers "counts" as a prayer discipline because they are not the active parties.

All of these reflections have perplexed me, but from them I have reached a tentative conclusion. Prayer is deliberately and conscientiously living life in relation to God. In this life, we think of problems, needs, and blessings, and we always see them through the perspective of our faith. I would submit that however we think, speak, and live Godwardly, that is a form of prayer. If I am right, we may pray more or less than we think we do. But we must remember that prayers are not validated by totaling up minutes in a specific form of activity. Prayer is a gift.

*2–How much time should we spend in prayer?*

Part of the answer here depends on how we define prayer. However, for purposes of this discussion, we will consider "formal" times of private prayer.

Nothing in the New Testament lays down divine requirements for the length of a prayer, and the evidence is ambiguous. Jesus prayed all night (Luke 6:12). Anna remained in the temple, "worshiping with fasting and prayer night and day" (Luke 2:37). Paul spoke of the widows who prayed day and night (1 Tim. 5:6). These instances certainly challenge us, but then, the Lord's Prayer can be prayed in less than a minute.

Many Christians have spoken of hours spent in daily prayer, even confessing that without such devotion it would be impossible for them to serve God as they do. Other powerful Christians have not practiced such extended times of prayer. Dangers lie in extremes either way. Extensive time in prayer may limit the amount of Christian "doing," but too little time in prayer may deny the necessary reliance on God. Since Christians are possessed of various gifts, we may appropriately apply this idea of giftedness to the practice of prayer. Some are deeply immersed in private prayer, while others find their Christian service manifested in other ways. The church needs people who are gifted in both ways.

Christians who are serious about prayer often are aware of a difficulty attending to their prayer lives. There is so much to pray about that we could spend all our waking hours in prayer. We can pray for every detail of our personal lives, confessing, asking for forgiveness and help, dealing with temptations, requesting wisdom; in short, laying every aspect of our inner and outer selves before God. Then there are prayers for others—for our families, our friends, our community, and those in the wider world. Beyond this circle of awareness, everyone we know and everyone we don't know in the whole human race has needs as well.

You see the problem. We have to stop somewhere. But where do we draw the line? I cannot answer this question for others; indeed, I struggle to answer it for myself. We must delimit ourselves in some way. God certainly understands.

This brings us to another problem that may surface: praying out of guilt, as if God will "get us" if we don't pray enough or correctly. We must beware lest our view of prayer conceal the feeling that only by praying properly can we earn divine approval. If we really want to walk the guilt road, we can tread it with regard to many aspects of living Christianly, not just regarding prayer. I would suggest we decide how and when we will pray and then do it joyfully, forgetting any concept of winning God's favor by our prayers. As we pray we can continue to ask God's guidance in the matter.

Often our circumstances help determine what we are able do in formal prayer times. Responsibilities abound at home, at work, with family, in the community, even with church activities. We may be fortunate to squeeze out a few minutes each day. For such people, this entire discussion seems irrelevant. But then there may come refreshing times of extended prayer, say on a long solo auto journey on sparsely traveled roads. We do the best we can.

We must be careful not to assume that the more minutes we spend in formal prayer, the better Christians we are. This attitude can lead to spiritual pride, and we remember what Jesus said about prideful prayer in the case of the Pharisee (Luke 18:9–14).

Of course, we must return to the fact that formal times of prayer may not be all the praying we do. Still, there is wisdom in recognizing that if we don't have set times of formal prayer, we may neglect praying altogether.

*3–What is the acceptable posture for prayer?*

We must first recognize that the posture of the heart is the prime concern when we pray. The situation of the body can certainly bear a relation to the condition of the heart, but we would be amiss to insist God has certain approved postures that we must assume before he will hear our prayers. Even if we made this assumption, there would be people who, because of bodily infirmity, could not comply. Should one assume they therefore could not pray? It is a poor faith that holds that only prayers from certain bodily postures would be valid.

In Scripture, we find references to prayers uttered from many postures, and no biblical mandate demands any particular one. We find prayers uttered while standing, while kneeling, while prostrate, and with hands raised. One might also pray sitting, or reclining, or while walking. If one's life is characterized by ceaseless prayer, then many postures will be involved.

Nonetheless, there are some things to consider regarding posture. Whatever our posture at a given time, we might well reflect on why we have chosen that posture and whether it has any spiritual meaning or significance. Are there postures that mostly aptly reflect our attitude toward God? Are there those that would enhance our prayers? Which best promote focus and concentration? Are there those that would detract from the prayer (most commonly, lying in bed at night, during which time we fall asleep)? Also, is there any significance in the testimony a given posture might bear to other people? For example, some would suggest that the humility they find suggested by kneeling may indicate man's fallen state.

Note: I am including the following ideas for consideration, not because I have definite answers to them.

*4–Should women lead prayer when in a mixed group?*

Let me begin by expressing a bias. From my experience in hearing women pray, I have concluded that they pray better than men. Their prayers often are more personal, more practical, and less formal. They seem more heartfelt and more related to the nitty-gritty of life. I am not making any assumption here about the heart relation of either sex to God, but only sharing an observation for what it is worth.

Three New Testament texts come to mind. First Corinthians 11:5 speaks of a woman praying or prophesying. I am assuming this was the same Lord's Day meeting about which Paul speaks in the latter chapters or 1 Corinthians. Some disagree with this and suggest the reference is to other occasions on which Christians had come together. Whatever the case, the women were praying when men were present.

The two texts that have engendered the most controversy on this issue are 1 Corinthians 14:33–34 ("As in all the churches of the saints, the women should keep silent in the churches.") and 1 Timothy 2:11–12. ("Let a woman learn in silence with all submissiveness. I permit no woman to teach or to have authority over men; she is to keep silent."). Most people agree that both texts speak of the Lord's Day meeting of the Christians. It is also generally agreed that the texts do not require *absolute* silence; otherwise, we would lack sopranos and altos in our singing. Just when, then, were women to remain silent? There are passionately held differences on this point, some of which are based on careful interpretation of Scripture, and some of which are based on tradition and custom. In my opinion, Paul was discussing, in both cases, abuses in worship. In 1 Corinthians, he demanded silence from three parties: the tongues speakers, the prophets, and the women. I believe he spoke of women who were disruptive, which I believe was a particular problem in Corinth. This disruption probably also involved lack of a proper regard for the husband–wife relationship. I also believe that men who were guilty of the same abuses also would be told by the apostle to be silent.

I am of the same persuasion with regard to 1 Timothy. In this text, both men and women were bidden to proper conduct. Verse 12 is teaching a woman should not teach when it involved seizing authority over men. In other words, the two items in the verse both refer to the same thing, not to two different things.

On the basis of this evidence, I conclude the New Testament has no prohibition of a woman leading prayer, and indeed indicates that many did. However, in the Lord's Day meeting she was to observe proper decorum and respect, and if she did not, she was bidden to silence. Paul does not say this in all his letters, but only, apparently, in those where the church had problems (Corinth and Ephesus).

I claim no infallibility on these issues, and I recognize there will be disagreements. It is important for all to be guided by Christian teaching, not by cultural and religious bias, whatever side of the issue one takes. It is also of surpassing importance to keep in mind the unity of the church and the sensitivities of members of a given congregation. Doing a thing that is right at one level could actually become a wrong at another level.

### 5–What value do the Old Testament psalms of lament have for Christian prayer?

In this book, we have not gone to the Old Testament for prayer instruction for the reasons indicated in chapter 4. But since about one-third of the Psalms are lamentations (cf. 22, 39, 44, 55, 69, 88), people often ask whether these form a viable model for Christian prayer since every life has its share of occasions for lament. How could these prayers not be appropriate when they were acceptable in ancient Israel *and* since they fit our lives?

There is something to be said for honesty when we speak to God, even when the result is complaint. Of course, nothing is concealed from him, so why should we pretend things are well when we are convinced they are not? I suspect God would rather have an honest expression of our hearts than approaches cloaked in pious pretense. If we carry our burdens to the great Physician, he may not remove the external trouble, and he often did not in these psalms. But he can transform our reactions and reinforce in us the greater view that tells us the final word for Christians is not defeat, but victory.

In the psalms of lament, the poet, when all else seems to fail, always can rely on God's steadfast love. That was great comfort. For Christians, this love comes incarnate in Jesus. It is because of the resurrection that Christians can rise above every seeming defeat. That may be why laments such as those in the Psalter are hardly a part of New Testament prayers. The disciples did not have a silly optimism that ignored problems— Jesus was risen, and so could his people be. The Israelite may have conceived God's future in shadowy ways, but followers of Jesus have the clear vision of the Lord who has ascended to heaven, and he pours out his Spirit, providing a strength that the ancient Israelites did not have in such fullness.

If Christians wish to complain in prayer, then why shouldn't they? But they also realize that the very center of their faith affords an unassailable victory and know that they live as "overcomers."

*6–What about "listening" to God in prayer?*

The difficulty here is in not knowing exactly what is meant by this expression. To the best of my knowledge, the New Testament does not describe such a phenomenon. However, if prayer seeks an answer and an answer comes, we probably had better listen. The danger, of course, is that we may hear what we want to hear, and that the voice may not be God but our inner self. We do seek answers to our prayers, but "listening" often implies some vague beyond. Nonetheless, there may be insights and understandings that come to us as we pray, and we should always be open to them. God will certainly give us what he wants us to have.

*7–What about fasting and prayer?*

Since fasting is mentioned twice in the activities of the early church (Acts 13:2–3; 14:23) and was a part of Jewish piety (cf. Luke 3:27), we frequently hear people ask if it should be a part of today's Christian practice. Jesus gave instructions forbidding ostentatious fasting, done to impress men (Matt. 6:1, 16–18). John's disciples fasted, but, at least on the occasion under consideration in Mark 2:18, Jesus' disciples did not. The Master defended them on the premise that kingdom celebration (cf. Mark 1:5) was a time of joy, not of sadness. When Jesus, "the bridegroom," left them, then they would fast.

There are several references to fasting in the Old Testament, but the only fast imposed on all Israelites was on the Day of Atonement (Lev. 26; Acts 27:9). There are no obligatory fasts levied upon the church, and, as we have noted, there are only two New Testament references to it as a church practice. Both are associated with prayer. Acts 13:2 indicates fasting left the church in Antioch open to divine guidance; the citation in 14:23 relates to the appointments of elders in several churches and to the need for them to be steadfast amidst persecution.

So what about prayer and fasting today? If practiced, fasting should be a voluntary activity, whether individually or collectively. I would hold that those who fast should know why they are fasting. The Bible is remarkably silent on the reasons, save for fasts that occur in times of penitence or mourning. Beyond Scripture, several reasons have been suggested for the practice:

a—to practice discipline in one area of life, which will enhance discipline in others

b—to cause one to be more sensitive to God, or to heighten religious consciousness

c—to reinforce the supplications expressed in prayer

d—to create focus on spiritual matters by laying aside certain needs of the body

If one chooses fasting with a clear understanding of the reasons behind the practice, he or she must be careful to avoid thinking it is an act of merit, causing one to be more deserving of God's attention and blessings. One can be just as fine a Christian and never fast as one can be who practices the custom.

### 8—What about prayer requests?

It is common, in prayer groups, for the prayer itself to be preceded by a call for prayer requests. In the following prayer, those for whom prayers have been requested are named again, and their concerns and joys are specified again as well. Sometimes the prayer leader adds further commentary.

This is a good practice. It shows faith in the power of prayer, and it underlines the importance of Christian caring in community. Nonetheless, there are some matters to keep in mind on such occasions:

a—The nature of this format will rule out some petitions, since they are not appropriate for such a public occasion. Thus, prayer request times should be balanced by times of private prayer, or prayer in small groups where there is such intimacy these matters can come before the Father in a corporate way.

b—When the details of specific prayer requests are described in advance, it seems unnecessary to mention them again. However, this is not a major issue.

c—Often these prayers are for people unknown to most in the group. It is hard to know how to pray in such cases.

d–The requested prayers may not be matters for which one can conscientiously pray. Wayne Jacobsen, in a fine article on this subject, cites an occasion when, after a certain prayer request, he said, "I don't think I can pray for that." Mouths dropped open, but he explained that he could not ask for things he did not think it was God's will to grant. He notes that some of these prayer requests are fundamentally selfish, even attempting to turn God away from his intents to the intents of the petitioner. His point is well-made and needs to be taken to heart in these prayer request situations.

*9. How long should we keep praying for the same thing?*

Many people keep a "prayer list," which functions as a reminder of prayer needs. This list likely includes the sick, those with spiritual problems, troubled marriages, etc. As needs are perceived or prayers requested, they are added to the list. Consequently, the list may become quite long, and this raises certain questions. How often is it necessary to pray for the same thing? Doesn't one prayer carry the need to God? Why the need for repetition? When do we drop a name or item from our list? In this last instance, many Christians feel a sense of guilt when they cease praying for a particular situation.

I doubt if there is any definitive answer to this dilemma. All people must seek their own procedures. However, we can offer some observations that may be helpful:

a–In praying for ourselves, the requests need to continue as long as the need continues. As a problem is resolved, or a temptation overcome, or a relationship mended, the answered prayer allows the request to cease. But since each of us is a bundle of needs, some kinds of prayers for our own spiritual lives will never end. The prayer relation needs to be reaffirmed daily to prevent a spiritual slipping away from the God who answers prayer.

b–Beyond requests, prayers of thanks are always appropriate. They may be stirred by immediate blessings, but since all we have comes from God, such prayers should be all-of-life activities.

c–In praying for others, we may discontinue prayers when the need no longer exists. The marriage is reconciled, the sick person healed, the decision is reached. Or, the situation may terminate in some less satisfactory way, in which case, the nature of our prayers may change.

d—We must avoid assuming that our prayers are essential for others, as if no resolution would come if we ceased them. It could be a short step to a kind of spiritual arrogance. One might say prayers for others are most valuable because they show that we care for them, but God will care for people no matter what, and his caring is infinitely greater than ours.

## Works Cited

Foster, Richard J. *Prayer: Finding the Heart's True Home*. San Francisco: Harper, 1992.

Jacobsen, Wayne. "Beyond Prayer Requests." *Leadership* 22 (Fall 2001), 48–52.

Johnson, Luke Timothy. *The Gospel of Luke*. Collegeville, MN: Liturgical Press, 1991.

Lewis, C. S. *Letters to Malcolm: Chiefly on Prayer*. San Diego: Harcourt, 1992.

_____. *The Problem of Pain*. San Francisco: Harper, 1996.

_____. *The Screwtape Letters*. San Francisco: Harper, 1996.

Marshall, I. Howard. *The Gospel of Luke*. Grand Rapids: Eerdmans, 1978.

Martin, Ralph P. *Word Biblical Commentary: James*. Waco: Word Books, 1988.

Nolland, John. *Word Biblical Commentary: Luke 9:21-18:34*. Dallas: Word Books, 1993.

# Also Available

*Living God's Love*
*An Invitation to Christian Spirituality*

by Gary Holloway & Earl Lavender

176 pages, $12.99 • ISBN 0-9748441-2-8

A simple, practical introduction
to the classic spiritual disciplines.
A wonderful tool for study groups,
prayer groups, and classes.

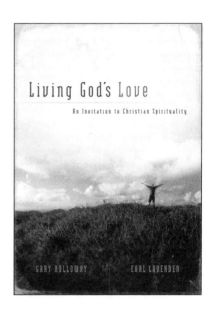

*"Our world is hungry for a life-giving way of life. That is what
Jesus offered—and offers still.* Living God's Love *makes that way
real and alive and accessible to real-world people."*

**JOHN ORTBERG**, AUTHOR OF *THE LIFE YOU'VE ALWAYS WANTED*

*"At last: a book that brings the essential subject of spiritual formation down
to earth. Clear, reverent, practical, and warm—I'll give this book to people in
my church to help them get on a healthy path of authentic Christian living."*

**BRIAN MCLAREN**, AUTHOR OF *A NEW KIND OF CHRISTIAN*

Available through your favorite bookstore
Or call toll free 1·877·816-4455

*Pilgrim Heart*
*The Way of Jesus in Everyday Life*

by Darryl Tippens

224 pages, $14.99   ISBN 0-9767790-7-2

This book invites you to consider
afresh the way of Jesus in light of
practices that have proven to transform
lives for two thousand years.

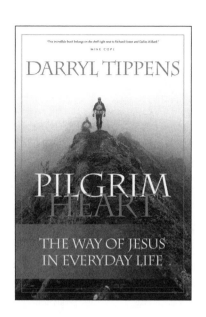

"Pilgrim Heart *is a vivid invitation to the moveable feast of Christian spirituality.*
*Serving as a warm and wise host, Darryl Tippens not only lucidly outlines the spiritual*
*disciplines, but introduces his readers to classical and contemporary companions in the*
*way, from St. Augustine to Henri Nouwen. His book is tasty, substantial, and lifegiving.*
*Bon appetit!"*

RODNEY CLAPP, AUTHOR OF *TORTURED WONDERS:*
*CHRISTIAN SPIRITUALITY FORPEOPLE, NOT ANGELS*

"*These words from Darryl Tippens—words that spotlight the* "attractive, challenging,
*and dramatically life-changing" path of Christ—are warm, deep, and accessible. This*
*incredible book belongs on the shelf right next to Richard Foster and Dallas Willard.*"

MIKE COPE, AUTHOR OF *RIGHTEOUSNESS INSIDE OUT*

Study Guide $5.99
ISBN 978-0-89112-552-5
One free with purchase of 8 or more
copies of *Pilgrim Heart*

Available through your favorite bookstore
Or call toll free 1·877·816-4455

Thin Places

*An Evangelical Journey into Celtic Christianity*

by Tracy Balzer

176 pages   $12.99 paper   ISBN 0-89112-513-2

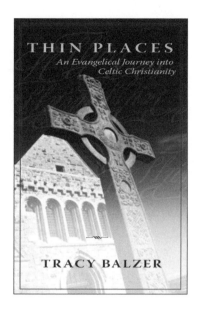

Thin Places introduces contemporary Christians to the great spiritual legacy of the early Celts, a legacy that has remained undiscovered or inaccessible for many evangelical Christians. It provides ways for us to learn from this ancient faith expression, applying fresh and lively spiritual disciplines to our own modern context.

"Thin Places *promises to wed evangelical piety to Celtic spirituality. We are all pilgrims in search of thin places; if we are too busy for thin places, we need to slow down. Tracy Balzer's splendid book will help each of us.*"

SCOT MCKNIGHT, PROFESSOR IN RELIGIOUS STUDIES, NORTH PARK UNIVERSITY;
AUTHOR OF *PRAYING WITH THE CHURCH* AND *EMBRACING GRACE*

"Thin Places *will be a great blessing to pilgrims on the Christian journey. It probes deep dimensions of the spiritual life, and deals with profound spiritual realities in an engaging and clarifying way. May the Lord anoint this gift to the world!*"

ROBERT MULHOLLAND, ASBURY THEOLOGICAL SEMINARY;
AUTHOR OF *THE DEEPER JOURNEY: THE SPIRITUALITY OF DISCOVERING YOUR TRUE SELF*

"*This is more than a book—it's an excursion to the land of the Celts full of 'aha' experiences of God, so opposite our contemporary culture but so crucial if we're to abide in Christ moment by moment.*"

JAN JOHNSON, AUTHOR OF *WHEN THE SOUL LISTENS* AND *ENJOYING THE PRESENCE OF GOD*

Available through your favorite bookstore
Or call toll free 1·877·816-4455